Learning from the Gosho: The Eternal Teachings of Nichiren Daishonin

by Daisaku Ikeda

ISBN: 978-1-932911-39-8

Copyright © 1997 The Soka Gakkai
Published by World Tribune Press
All rights reserved
10 9
Printed in the United States of America

Daisaku Ikeda was born in Tokyo on January 2, 1928. A graduate of Fuji Junior College, he joined Soka Gakkai in 1947. He became president of Soka Gakkai International in 1975, and honorary president of Soka Gakkai in 1979.

Mr. Ikeda has also founded several institutions, including Soka University, Soka Women's Junior College, Soka Junior and Senior High Schools, Soka Elementary School, Soka Kindergarten, Min-On Concert Association, Institute of Oriental Philosophy and the Fuji Art Museum and the Boston Research Center.

A poet laureate, Mr. Ikeda has received awards and honorary degrees from institutions and universities around the world, including the United Nations Peace Award. He has made numerous proposals on peace, disarmament, culture and education, and is also the author of many books ranging from Buddhist studies, novels and poetry to essays and travel diaries. His writings have been translated into more than a dozen languages.

Quotations from the Lotus Sutra have been taken from *The Lotus Sutra*, trans. Burton Watson, (New York: Columbia University Press, 1993). They are referenced in the following format: (LS2, 24), which, in this example, refers to the second chapter, p. 24.

Quotations from the series *The Major Writings of Nichiren Daishonin* are referenced in the following format: (MW-3, 78), which, in this example, refers to volume 3, p. 78.

Contents

'Gift of an Unlined Robe' (1)	7
'Gift of an Unlined Robe' (2)	17
'The Izu Exile' (1)	28
'The Izu Exile' (2)	38
'The Opening of the Eyes' (1)	49
'The Opening of the Eyes' (2)	59
'The One Essential Phrase' (1)	73
'The One Essential Phrase' (2)	83
'Letter to Ko-ama Gozen' (1)	95
'Letter to Ko-ama Gozen' (2)	107
'Letter to the Mother of Oto Gozen' (1)	122

'Letter to the Mother of Oto Gozen' (2)	132
'Letter to Lord Toki'	143
'A Letter of Condolence'	154
'Two Letters to Ueno-ama Gozen'	165
'The Ultimate Teaching Affirmed by All Buddhas of Past, Present and Future'	178
'Reply to Myoho Bikuni' (1)	191
'Reply to Myoho Bikuni' (2)	205
'Reply to Myoho Bikuni' (3)	219
'Happiness in This World'	233

'Gift of an Unlined Robe' (1)

The Gosho,[1] the collected writings of Nichiren Daishonin, elucidates the means for all people to attain enlightenment. It is the eternal teaching. The Gosho is a scripture of boundless hope. As long as we continue to study the Gosho and put its teachings into practice, we definitely will never become deadlocked.

Some Gosho, of course, are very doctrinal and complex. But we do not necessarily have to understand all of the Daishonin's writings. The important thing is to have a keen desire to read the Gosho and to expose our lives, even for just a short time each day, to Nichiren Daishonin's spirit.

Having such a seeking mind enables us to securely anchor our lives to the orbit of true happiness, to the path of attaining Buddhahood in this lifetime. And it becomes the engine for advancing kosen-rufu.

To meet the requests of members, for one year I lectured on "Expedient Means" and "The Life Span of the Thus Come One," the second and sixteenth chapters of the Lotus Sutra. Now begins a series of lectures on the Gosho with the aim of helping members strengthen themselves in the two ways of practice and study.

I will take up Gosho individually, and may devote more than one installment to particular writings. In the case of longer Gosho, I may limit myself to discussing only a portion. In all instances, my purpose will be to clarify the humanistic philosophy of Buddhism.

We will begin with a two-part study of the Gosho "Gift of an Unlined Robe."[2]

> **I have received the unlined robe that you graciously sent.** (*Gosho Zenshu*, p. 1514)

This letter is dated a little more than a year after the Daishonin retired to Mount Minobu. He had received a gift of a robe from a couple, followers of his whom he had not yet met. An unlined robe is a light garment suitable for use in hot weather.

The couple must have been concerned about the difficulty of the Daishonin's life in the mountains. In their gift, we can sense a real human tenderness. Theirs was an offering made with sincerity.

The Daishonin may have used the brief interval before the couple's messenger set out on his return journey to take up his brush and compose a letter of thanks. This is the letter.

While the names of the husband and wife who received this letter are not known, it is surmised that they may have been relations of the Nanjo family, or followers living in Kamakura. Since they had not yet met the Daishonin directly, they probably were not central figures among his followers. From the contents of the letter, however, it is apparent that they were carrying through with steadfast faith.

The nameless people count most. The essence of Buddhism shines in their down-to-earth efforts to make faith manifest in daily life.

The Daishonin replied to the sincerity of this couple with his own sincerity. This letter abundantly conveys his spirit in this regard. Let us always bear this spirit in mind.

The letter is pervaded with the compassion of the Daishonin, who assures them that their sincerity is definitely known to all Buddhas, and that they are certain to attain Buddhahood. Their offering was a robe and yet more than just a robe; in the gift, the Daishonin perceived the heart and very life of his followers.

I know of no other religious figure who wrote such considerate letters of appreciation in response to each offering received. Nearly all of the Daishonin's personal letters to his followers were written in thanks for offerings.

The Daishonin replied from his heart to others' hearts. He replied to sincerity with great sincerity — and with lightning speed. This was also the spirit of Josei Toda, the second Soka Gakkai president. The Soka Gakkai has developed to such an extent because we have maintained this spirit to this day.

Followers reading the Daishonin's letters must have been deeply moved by his warmth. More than a few continued to advance with the Daishonin despite great persecution. That was because of the heart-to-heart bonds that existed between him and each of his followers.

It is the same in the SGI. The SGI is strong not because of its organization but because we are creating invisible bonds of the heart.

A Great Spiritual Revolution

> In the past, in a country called Kirokoku, old people were abandoned. In Japan, today, the Lotus Sutra's votary is cast away.
>
> Since the country's appearance, there have been seven reigns of heavenly gods and five generations of earthly gods. It was then that the 100 reigns of human sovereign began. There have been ninety reigns since Emperor Jimmu. And already sixty reigns have passed since Buddhism was introduced to the country during the reign of Emperor Kimmei [the twenty-ninth] more than 700 years ago.
>
> During this time, there have been countless parent-murderers, enemies of the emperor, mountain bandits and pirates. But I have never heard of someone who was hated as much as I, Nichiren, on account of the Lotus Sutra. Some have been hated by the ruler but not by the people, or have been hated by priests but not by lay people, or have been hated by men but not by women, or have been hated by the ignorant but not by the wise.

But I am hated by the people even more than by the ruler, by laymen and laywomen even more than by monks and nuns, by the wise even more than by the ignorant, and by the good even more than by the wicked. My case is thus entirely without precedent. Nor is it likely that anyone in later ages will receive such treatment. (*Gosho Zenshu*, p. 1514)

In Kirokoku the elderly were discarded to reduce the number of mouths to feed. Buddhist scriptures speak of lands in which it was customary for the elderly to be treated poorly. One sutra relates an episode where a kingdom puts an end to this cruel custom. A minister, in violation of the law of the land, does not turn out his aged father but secretly maintains him. Later, the kingdom is visited by a crisis and no one knows what to do. The land is saved from calamity by the wisdom of the aged father who had been in hiding. Thereupon the ruler changes the laws and makes it so that the elderly are respected.

Nichiren Daishonin says that just as this ancient country had discarded its wise people, Japan has thrown away the votary of the Lotus Sutra. No country is more foolish than one that discards its people of wisdom, who can save it from disaster.

The death in prison of Tsunesaburo Makiguchi, the Soka Gakkai's founding president, amounted to wartime Japan's having "thrown away the Lotus Sutra's votary." Japan, therefore, was headed for ruin.

As the Daishonin says in this writing, no one has been as hated as he on account of the Lotus Sutra. Although he was fighting for the people's happiness, he was hated even by the people. This might seem unreasonable, but such is the lot of all those who seek to open a new path forward.

"If the Mystic Law is correct," President Toda was once asked, "then why is it so difficult to spread?" He explained:

> Precisely because it is correct, people have a hard time accepting it. For example, it's correct for children to be dutiful toward their parents. But are you truly so considerate of your parents? It's something in which people rarely succeed. We may not necessarily study hard even though we know that it's important. And people who are broke may go out and squander their paychecks on alcohol even though they know it's the wrong thing to do. Similarly, Nichiren Daishonin teaches that the more correct a teaching, the more enemies it will have.

Not only do people fail to do what is correct, they tend to react emotionally and negatively toward a person of justice. This is human nature.

In particular, arrogant authorities cannot bear to have anyone stand up to them and speak out for justice. That's because they regard themselves as superior to everyone. This is an unchanging principle.

> **As a result, during the more than twenty years from when I was 32 [when he established his teaching] until now, at 54, I have been driven out of temples, I have been expelled from my place of residence, my parents and relatives have been harassed, I have been**

> attacked at night, I have encountered battles, I have been vilified countless times, I have been struck and injured, my disciples have been killed, I have nearly been beheaded, and twice been sent into exile.

"During these more than twenty years, I have never known even an hour or a moment of peace," the Daishonin says. He lived this way for us. How merciful! His was a great struggle for spiritual revolution more intense than any battle.

From the time the Daishonin established his teaching at 32, great persecutions rained down upon him. Still, he never retreated a single step.

To elaborate on the persecutions that the Daishonin touches on in this writing, which represent only a portion of the difficulties he underwent: He was driven away from Seicho-ji [the temple where he had received his initial training as a priest, and where he proclaimed the establishment of his teaching]; he was chased away from his birthplace of Awa; his parents and relatives were made to suffer greatly; he was attacked at night while dwelling in a hermitage; he was attacked at Komatsubara; groundless rumors about him were spread; and he was the target of countless insults.

In the Komatsubara Persecution, the Daishonin's left arm was broken and he received a sword wound to his forehead. Also, his disciples were killed. When Hei no Saemon came to arrest him, the Daishonin was struck by Sho-bo (also called Shofu-bo) with a sutra scroll, and in the Tatsunokuchi Persecution he was nearly beheaded. In addition, he was twice exiled, to Izu and to Sado Island.

Yet the Daishonin continued to stand up bravely. "Still I am not discouraged" (MW-1, 166), he says. "I rejoiced, [having] long expected it to come to this" (MW-1, 175). "It is all just as I expected" (MW-1, 36).

This was all for the people — he underwent everything on our behalf. He sought nothing for himself. Had he desired to lead a peaceful and tranquil life, he could certainly have done so. And he plainly understood that once he stood up he would encounter great persecution. Nevertheless, the Daishonin dared to stand up.

In this letter, where he lists persecutions he had undergone, there is not the least note of bitterness or complaint. Rather, the Daishonin took tremendous pride in having undergone great persecution. In this, we can sense the heartbeat of the indomitable lion king.

We are the Daishonin's disciples. We carry on his great struggle. This is the greatest possible honor. Compared with the great persecutions the Daishonin underwent, to be called a few names hardly amounts to anything.

President Toda wrote of the period during World War II when the militarists were bent on ruthlessly suppressing all dissenting voices:

> The surprise and confusion of believers and the perplexity of those affiliated with the head temple were such that it was comical to hear and embarrassing to imagine. President Makiguchi, myself and all the members with us were prohibited from making pilgrimages to the head temple, and far and wide we were vilified as

enemies of the nation. Such absurdity, while a reflection of the conditions of the times, was even laughable.

And those put in prison were also pathetic. Some saw their businesses collapse. And their families were hounded by debt collectors or simply unable to provide for themselves for want of a livelihood. The families they left behind were, just as much as the prisoners, at a loss for what to do.

Consequently, the families abandoned faith or began to doubt. This was because they lacked confidence and had only a dim grasp of the Daishonin's teachings. And one by one, those who were imprisoned abandoned their faith, too. They were spineless people. They lacked courage and had weak faith. This was the pitiful plight of those who failed to recognize the Daishonin as the original Buddha.

Even amid such circumstances, Mr. Toda felt deep appreciation toward his mentor, President Makiguchi, to whom in a memorial he would later say, "In your vast and boundless compassion, you allowed me to come with you even to prison." This eloquently sums up their solemn, magnificent relationship as mentor and disciple.

As expressed in even this short Gosho, the Daishonin was at once dauntlessly strong toward arrogant authorities and infinitely kind toward people of sincerity. These are both manifestations of his compassion. This sums up Nichiren Daishonin's sublime humanism.

1. The term *Gosho* can be used in either the singular or the plural.

2. "Hitoe Sho," written in August 1275 when Nichiren Daishonin was 54.

'Gift of an Unlined Robe' (2)

The fourth volume of the Lotus Sutra states, "hatred and jealousy toward this sutra abound even when the Thus Come One is in the world" (LS10, 164). The fifth volume explains that the Lotus Sutra "will face much hostility in the world and be difficult to believe" (LS14, 207). It may be that the Great Teacher T'ien-t'ai never read these passages with his life. That's because the Lotus Sutra was universally believed and accepted by the people of his day. Nor in all likelihood was the Great Teacher Dengyo capable of living these words, because the conditions of the time in which he lived did not match those described by the passage "[since hatred and jealousy toward this sutra abound even when the Thus Come One is in the world,] how much more will this be so after his passing?" (LS10, 164).

If Nichiren had not appeared in the country of Japan, these golden words of the Buddha would have been

> in vain. The testimony of Many Treasures (Taho) Buddha would not have amounted to anything. And the words of all Buddhas of the ten directions would have become lies. In the more than 2,220 years since the Buddha passed away, never before in India, China or Japan has there been someone to whom the words of the sutra, "It will face much hostility in the world and be difficult to believe," have applied. If Nichiren had not appeared, the Buddha's words would have withered. (*Gosho Zenshu*, p. 1514)

"Buddhism exists because I exist"— this is the Daishonin's immense conviction. The Buddha's words, in a sense, became true precisely because the Daishonin single-handedly underwent great persecution.

To prove the proposition "Buddhism is true," the Daishonin deliberately drew out negative forces and challenged them. Without such a great struggle, even the most outstanding scripture would, in the end, be no more than a book. Even the most profound sutra would be merely words. The sutra's words only become Buddhism, only become a genuine religion, when they are put to the test in life.

This year, once again, we have commemorated April 2 [the anniversary of the passing of the second Soka Gakkai president, Josei Toda]. My mentor, President Toda, whom I will remember for all eternity, dedicated his entire life to proving the truth of Nichiren Daishonin's words. Through his life, in the real world, he began to make a reality of kosen-rufu, which had for 700 years been only theory.

The Daishonin says, "If Nichiren had not appeared, the Buddha's words would have withered." The spirit to not allow the words of the original Buddha, Nichiren Daishonin, to have been in vain is the fundamental spirit of the Soka Gakkai. This was the spirit of Tsunesaburo Makiguchi, and of Josei Toda. And this is the spirit of a disciple.

President Makiguchi deeply lamented the state of the priesthood. Solely concerned with defending its own interests, it had bowed before the military authorities and become mired in slander. "Isn't this the time when we should remonstrate with the state?" he cried. "What are you afraid of?" And he went on to become a martyr for the Daishonin's teachings.

President Toda once reminisced about his mentor, saying:

> The last time I saw President Makiguchi alive was in 1943. It was on the second floor of the Metropolitan Police Station. He was about to be taken to Tokyo Prison in Sugamo, and I was to follow later. I told the department officer that I wanted to bid him farewell, and I went to where he was.

> When I met him there, I just looked at his face and wept. I could not speak. The last words I said to him were, "Please take care."

> Later, I was unaware that President Makiguchi had died. I shall never forget the day — January 8, 1945 — when I was summoned before the preliminary judge for the very first time and told bluntly, "Makiguchi's dead." I

> just stood there stunned, unable even to weep. When I returned to my cell, I cried my heart out.
>
> I had never experienced such grief as I felt at that moment. Then and there, I resolved: "I will show the world. I will prove beyond a doubt the righteousness of my mentor! If I were to adopt a pseudonym, I'd use the 'Count of Monte Cristo' [the hero of Alexandre Dumas' novel, who was unjustly incarcerated]. With such resolve, I will achieve something great to repay him."
>
> President Makiguchi has not received the recognition that is his due. And I am determined to dedicate the rest of my life to proving the righteousness of my mentor's actions.[1]

Every year when April 2 comes around, my heart is filled with exactly the same feelings toward my mentor, President Toda.

Today Mr. Makiguchi's name is known throughout the world. A suburb of São Paulo, Brazil, for example, has opened a Tsunesaburo Makiguchi Highway. And the Brazilian city of Curitiba is building a Tsunesaburo Makiguchi Park and also a Josei Toda Boulevard.

How it must delight President Toda for his mentor to be so honored. It almost seems to me as though I can see his smiling face in the blue skies of spring.

> Under these circumstances, I maintain my life with snow for food as did Su Wu[2] when he was imprisoned. And I pass my time clad in a straw raincoat

like Li Ling.[3] At times when there are no fruits or berries available in the trees of these mountains where I reside, I may go two or three days without eating. And once when my deerskin garment was torn, I went unclad for three or four months.

You have for some reason taken pity on such a person and, even though we have not yet met, sent a robe with which I might clothe myself. For this I am infinitely grateful. (*Gosho Zenshu*, pp. 1514–15)

More than a year had passed since the Daishonin took up residence deep in the recesses of Mount Minobu. These were the conditions under which he was living. Su Wu and Li Ling were Chinese generals of antiquity who, though they exerted themselves on behalf of the country, were captured by enemies and wound up leading highly constricted lives.

While eating snow, wearing crude garments made of straw, and living in a small hut, the Daishonin led the movement for the widespread propagation of the Mystic Law. Living with him were his disciples, and they had occasional "visits" from birds and deer.

In winter, it was extremely cold — so cold that they had trouble sleeping. They lacked sufficient food, and had neither miso nor salt in ample supply. It is said that the Daishonin gathered nuts and parsley and collected firewood to prepare food for himself and his disciples. It is also said that for clothing the Daishonin wore the skin of a deer that had died of natural causes.

By rights, the Daishonin ought to have been accorded the treatment due a teacher of the entire nation. But Japan repaid him only with persecution, so that he lived in want of even clothing and food.

Copious tears always welled up in President Toda's eyes when he read in the Gosho of the Daishonin's life under such circumstances. He would often remark: "The original Buddha suffered so much. No matter what happens, we who are his followers have to persevere. We have to make the Daishonin's immense compassion known to the world."

Moreover, the Daishonin, while living under such conditions, continued to raise and encourage his followers, leaving them Gohonzon and Gosho. He thus devoted himself resolutely to establishing the path for kosen-rufu in the Latter Day of the Law. His compassion truly knew no bounds! How fortunate we are to be his followers!

The Daishonin described his daily existence in the frankest terms. If it was cold, he would say it was cold. And if he was suffering from hunger, he would indicate it. A Buddha is not some special being. A Buddha is human through and through. President Toda often called him a "great common mortal." And he hated being referred to, with bated breath, as "the founder." Buddhism is not a religion that produces so-called living Buddhas. Rather, it enables ordinary people, just as they are, to manifest the light of supreme humanity.

Nichiren Daishonin, though experiencing extreme hardship himself, offered this unknown couple (to whom he addressed this Gosho) such sincere and warm encouragement. He did the same while in Izu and Sado. Though an exile, he was more concerned about the plight of others than about his own troubles.

Once when some of the Daishonin's followers visited him on Sado Island, a profoundly moving drama unfolded. They had made a long journey to inquire after the Daishonin's well-being. He met their concern with his own concern about their expenses for the return trip and even went so far as to borrow money from someone to give to them. Even facing the most difficult of circumstances, the Daishonin possessed the magnanimity and broad-mindedness to be most concerned about the welfare of others. In his conduct, we find true human strength and beauty.

A Sincere Offering Confers Immeasurable Benefit

> When I put on this robe and recite the Lotus Sutra before the Buddha, while the robe is only one, it clothes 69,384 Buddhas. This is because there are 69,384 characters in the Lotus Sutra. And each character is a golden Buddha.

> Therefore, these Buddhas will surely visit the two of you, husband and wife, who presented me with this robe and protect you as their followers.

> In this life, your sincere offering becomes a prayer for the fulfillment of your every desire and a treasure. At the time of your deaths it will become the moon, the

> sun, a path, a bridge, a father, a mother, an ox or a horse, a litter, a cart, a lotus flower, and a mountain, and will usher you into the pure land of Eagle Peak. Nam-myoho-renge-kyo, Nam-myoho-renge-kyo.
>
> Nichiren
>
> The eighth month of the first year of Kenji (1275)
>
> You should always meet with the wife of Toshiro and read this letter together. (*Gosho Zenshu*, p. 1515)

What a welcome promise the Daishonin makes! He says that the couple who has made this offering to the Lotus Sutra's votary will be protected by 69,384 Buddhas. Such a grand spectacle defies the imagination. With such protection over the three existences, what could they possibly have to fear?

Elsewhere he says, "The heart alone is what really matters." As the story of the boy who makes an offering of a mud pie to Shakyamuni and is later reborn as King Ashoka illustrates, the heart is indeed mysterious and inscrutable.

The Mystic Law elucidates the inscrutable workings of the heart. The doctrine of a life-moment possesses three thousand realms explains the immense power of the heart. A Buddha is someone who understands, on the most profound level, the workings and the power of the heart.

As stated in the passage of the Lotus Sutra, "They will enjoy peace and security in their present existence and good circumstances in future existences" (LS5, 99), the Daishonin assures the couple that they have absolutely nothing to fear in their present and future existences.

First, he says that in their present lives their offering will become a "prayer" and a "treasure." He thus indicates that, through the protective functions of all Buddhas, their sincere faith in offering a robe will become a cause for the fulfillment of all their desires and the accumulation of immense benefit.

Then, regarding the journey after death, he says that they will be protected by all Buddhas and need have no fear. Their faith in making this offering will become a "sun" and "moon" brightly illuminating their journey, as well as a "great path" and a "bridge" over which to make their way.

They will be gently led by the hand by a loving "mother" and "father." They can ride with composure on either an "ox" or a "horse," a "litter" or a "cart." And finally, they will board the "lotus flower" for Buddhas and bodhisattvas, and arrive at the "treasure mountain" — the pure land of Eagle Peak where the Buddha dwells.

For an offering of but a single unlined robe, the Daishonin promises eternal good fortune and benefit. This is because he perceives the sincerity with which the robe is imbued.

The unlined robe the couple sent was woven through and through with their sincerity. No doubt the Daishonin could sense this in its warmth and feel. How truly noble and pure were the hearts of this couple, who believed in and devoted themselves to the Daishonin at a time when the entire country was desperately trying to persecute him.

A person who has crossed the precipice of life and death many times understands true human worth. Neither power nor fame makes someone great. The light of true human greatness shines vividly among ordinary people who live straight and true, neither seeking honor nor craving wealth. One can well imagine the joy of the couple who received this letter.

Incidentally, the person mentioned in the postscript, "the wife of Toshiro," was a friend of Shijo Kingo's family.

The Daishonin concludes by urging the couple to gather with other followers and read this letter together. In modern terms, he is telling them to hold discussion meetings. As long as we continue to study the Gosho and discuss faith with our fellow members, there is no danger of our deviating from the correct path.

In just this brief postscript, the Daishonin touches on the vital point of carrying through with faith in unity with other believers in the Mystic Law. Such detailed consideration is characteristic of the Daishonin — it is the spirit of the original Buddha.

We need to treasure each person thoroughly. This is the spirit of the Gosho and of the SGI.

The Gosho is the jewel of humankind that crystallizes with diamond-like clarity the humanism of Nichiren Daishonin. Because this is an age of spiritual malaise, it is all the more important that we study the Gosho and return to the humanism of Nichiren Daishonin.

1. From Josei Toda's remarks at the eleventh memorial service for President Makiguchi (1954).

2. Su Wu (140–60 B.C.E.): A minister of Emperor Wu of the Former Han dynasty. In 100 B.C.E., the emperor sent Su Wu to demand that a northern tribe acknowledge fealty. Their chief had Su Wu seized and imprisoned in a cave, where he was forced to survive by eating snow.

3. Li Ling (d. 74 B.C.E.): A military commander during the Former Han dynasty. During battle, he was captured by barbarians and imprisoned. Emperor Wu mistakenly believed that he had revolted against the Han dynasty, and had his family killed.

'The Izu Exile' (1)

Appreciation Is the Wellspring of Humanity

Appreciation is what makes people truly human. The Japanese word for *thankful* (*arigatai*) originally indicated a rare or unusual condition, and later came to denote a sense of joyful appreciation at an uncommon occurrence.

Having a spirit of appreciation for someone from whose actions we benefit, a sense that "this is the rarest and noblest thing," produces in our hearts a feeling of pride and self-esteem: "I am worthy of receiving such goodness." It provides us with spiritual support to go on living.

I once heard an episode involving a young man on the verge of committing suicide. Someone trying to dissuade him from this course suggested that he first write letters to everyone to whom he owed thanks. When the youth thought about all the people he ought to write and realized how many had supported and helped him along the way, the power to go on living welled up within him.

A spirit of gratitude strengthens and elevates our lives. By contrast, the arrogance to take for granted the favors and help we have been fortunate enough to receive can make us mean and base — qualities, I fear, that could be said to characterize the Japanese today.

The Gosho we will now study[1] is a letter of appreciation that Nichiren Daishonin, the Buddha of the Latter Day of the Law, sent to the fisherman Funamori Yasaburo and his wife, whom he had met while exiled in Izu. He goes so far as to suggest that they are reincarnations of Shakyamuni who appeared in order to help him. The Daishonin was a person of the greatest appreciation and humanism.

> I have received rice dumplings wrapped in bamboo leaves, sake, dried rice, peppers, paper and other items from the messenger whom you took the trouble of sending. He also conveyed your message that this offering should be kept secret. I understand.
>
> On the twelfth day of the fifth month, having been exiled, I arrived at the harbor.[2] When I left the boat, still in suffering, and even before learning your name, you kindly took me into your care. What destiny brought us together? You might have been a votary of the Lotus Sutra in times past. Now, in the Latter Day of the Law, you were born as Funamori Yasaburo to take pity on me. Being a man, it was perhaps natural for you to act as you did, but your wife might have been less inclined to help me. Nevertheless, she

> gave me food, brought me water to wash my hands and feet and treated me with great concern. It is beyond me to fathom [this karmic relationship]; I can only describe it as wondrous.
>
> What caused you to believe in the Lotus Sutra and to make offerings to me during my more than thirty-day stay there? (MW-2 [2ND ED.], 54)

At the beginning, the Daishonin lists all the items he has received as offerings. He replies from the heart to the sincerity with which each item is imbued. He takes not even a single piece of wrapping paper for granted. This is the Buddha's spirit.

Again, regarding the message from the couple, who were anxious about the Daishonin's safety, he tells them, "I have received the message, and I understand." One can almost hear the Daishonin's gentle voice. In just the first few lines of the letter, he puts their minds at ease and completely embraces them in his compassion.

On May 12, 1261, Nichiren Daishonin was exiled to Izu as a criminal. It appears he was transported there aboard a small vessel escorted by just a few officers and oarsmen. It is believed that they set out from Kamakura harbor in the morning and neared the shore of Ito late in the day. The boat, bound for Ito harbor, drifted ashore in the harbor at Kawana, a short distance from Ito.

The Daishonin was no doubt exhausted from the long journey and may also have been seasick. The fisherman

Funamori Yasaburo came to the Daishonin's aid when he landed on the beach in his much beleaguered state.

For the next month, Yasaburo and his wife are said to have looked after the Daishonin, who subsequently went to the residence of the steward of the district, Ito Hachiro Zaemon. Yasaburo and his wife, with unwavering sincerity, secretly sent offerings there for the Daishonin. This Gosho is his letter of thanks.

Yasaburo and his wife may simply have been pure-hearted people who could not turn away when they saw someone having difficulties. Even so, the Daishonin's having encountered such benevolent people in his place of exile is extraordinary, and he expresses surprise.

Yasaburo and his wife were no doubt moved by the Daishonin's words. They probably thought to themselves in wonderment: "So in a past life we were votaries of the Lotus Sutra. And we have been living in this place in order to fulfill the promise we made then."

One can imagine them, having newly awakened to faith in the Lotus Sutra, smiling and discussing their sense of inspiration.

> I was hated and resented by the steward and people of the district even more than I was in Kamakura. Those who saw me scowled, while those who merely heard my name were filled with spite. And yet, though I was there in the fifth month when rice was scarce, you secretly fed me. It would almost seem as though my parents had been reborn in Kawana close to Ito in Izu Province. (MW-2 [2ND ED.], 54-55)

All his life, Nichiren Daishonin was hounded by the bad name pinned to him by jealous people. But while the calumny was severe in Kamakura, many followers there also knew the truth about him. Throughout Kamakura, the Daishonin's followers probably conducted a campaign of dialogue, telling people: "The priest Nichiren that we know is not the kind of person they say. There is no one more upright and gentle."

But in Izu he had neither disciples nor allies. So, when the Daishonin arrived there, having been made out to be a criminal by the authorities, malicious rumors spread uncontested. The villagers feared and hated the "evil priest" who had fallen in among them. Doubtless some felt that if they came upon the Daishonin they would do him in.

When the Soka Kyoiku Gakkai[3] was suppressed by the authorities more than fifty years ago, Tsunesaburo Makiguchi, Josei Toda and their families were also, in Mr. Toda's words, "condemned by the entire populace as enemies of the nation."[4]

Yasaburo and his wife were not misled by the rumors about the Daishonin. They observed his character with their own eyes and bravely protected him, becoming his shield.

Not only that, but at a time of year when rice was scarce, they prepared rice for the Daishonin and otherwise exerted themselves on his behalf with the utmost sincerity. The fifth month of the old lunar calendar, when this letter was written, probably fell within the rainy season. Moreover, the topography of the Izu area greatly limits how much land can be cultivated.

Yasaburo may have had to go fishing more often than usual and his wife must have had to scrimp to make ends meet. The Daishonin was aware of all of their efforts. With his one comment acknowledging that rice must have been very scarce, the weight of their painstaking toils must have instantly lightened.

As Buddhists, we need to be sensitive to other people's situations, to put out the "antennas of the heart," as it were. Such concern and sensitivity, which the Daishonin teaches here through his own example, are essential parts of the makeup of a Buddhist.

In this regard alone, it is plain that the members of the Nichiren Shoshu priesthood today, in their decadent conduct, are the exact opposite of the Daishonin. The opposite of the Buddha is the devil, the enemy of the Buddha. Nichiren Daishonin could not possibly condone the priesthood now, which has trampled on the sincere offerings people have made by the sweat of their brows.

Even while the Daishonin was with them, Yasaburo and his wife must have been impressed time and again by his delicate sensitivity. Their hearts must have brimmed with joy at the sincerity of the Daishonin, who responded to their kindness with heartfelt gratitude.

Even under the most adverse circumstances, the Daishonin always created allies through his conduct. Such a drama unfolded even during the Tatsunokuchi Persecution, when the military government, having failed to behead the Daishonin, had him taken to the residence of Lord Homma Rokuro Zaemon in Echi. There, the Daishonin ordered sake for the officers who had accompanied him from Kamakura and commended them on their labors through the night. Who has ever heard of a prisoner praising his arresting officers? And in this case, only a little while earlier the officers had been trying to have him beheaded.

Some had hated the Daishonin for many years. But his complete composure won him friends even among such people. Some wound up throwing down their Nembutsu beads and swearing to follow him.

Ultimately, Buddhism comes down to the person. I did not wait to place my trust in President Toda until *after* I had learned about the Daishonin's teachings. Rather, I came to trust Buddhism because I first believed in the person, Josei Toda.

Become Yasaburos of the Present Age

Incidentally, Kawana was a small village, and word of the Daishonin's arrival there must have spread quickly. But there was no great commotion. This was perhaps because Yasaburo had gained the trust and respect of the residents of the fishing village. Here again, the person was the all-important factor.

The Daishonin was always protected by the power of the people. Kosen-rufu is shouldered by ordinary people of sincerity, not by some faction of clever elites.

I hope men's division members, in particular, will become modern Funamori Yasaburos, commanding solid trust and credibility in their communities, and staunchly protecting the precious children of the Buddha who are advancing the work of kosen-rufu.

SGI Members Are Carrying Out the Work of the Buddhist Gods

The fourth volume of the Lotus Sutra states, "[If after I (Shakyamuni) have entered extinction there are those who can expound this sutra, I will send...monks and nuns and] men and women of pure faith, to offer alms to the teachers of the Law"(LS10, 168). The meaning of this sutra passage is that the heavenly gods and benevolent deities will assume various forms such as men and women and present offerings to help one who practices the Lotus Sutra. There can be no doubt that you and your wife were born as just such a man and woman of pure faith and now make offerings to the teacher of the Law, Nichiren.

Since I wrote to you in detail earlier, I will make this letter brief. (MW-2 [2ND ED.], 55)

Here, citing a passage from "The Teacher of the Law," the tenth chapter of the Lotus Sutra, the Daishonin praises Yasaburo and his wife as Buddhist gods. The "teacher of the Law" indicates Nichiren Daishonin specifically, but in a general sense it also applies to his followers, to each of us who practice and spread the Mystic Law. And the Daishonin says that the Buddhist gods assume a variety of forms in protecting us.

Buddhism is not abstract theory; concepts such as the Buddhist gods have concrete and immediate application to our everyday lives. Our fellow members function as Buddhist gods for us, and so should be highly treasured and appreciated.

Whenever we are suffering, whether due to sickness, accidents, natural disasters or some other cause, they come running straight away to offer encouragement. And when we have cause to rejoice, they join us in celebration. They pray to the Gohonzon with us, are always ready to discuss things, and join us in taking action. Isn't all this the work of our fellow SGI members? To have such friends is certainly the rarest good fortune.

One scholar says admiringly of the SGI, "In a world where people are indifferent to the plight of others, it's amazing to see people interacting so harmoniously."

Truly, as the saying goes, it is in times of need that we know our friends. The SGI is a wonderful gathering of good friends. Where else can such a rich world of mutual protection and encouragement — such a golden palace of the people — be found?

The Daishonin says that incalculable Buddhas, Bodhisattva Superior Practices (Jpn. Jogyo) and the other Bodhisattvas of the Earth, the bodhisattvas of the provisional teachings, King Brahma (Bonten), the gods of the sun and moon, the major and minor deities and all Buddhist gods protect those who firmly and wholeheartedly believe in the Lotus Sutra, watching over them just as the shadow follows the body (*Gosho Zenshu*, p. 1528).

In light of the Gosho, SGI members are precious and noble beings who carry out the work of all Buddhas, bodhisattvas and Buddhist gods. Therefore, let us by all means treasure our fellow members. Let us carry through with faith — filled with gratitude for our profound and mystic connections with one another.

1. "Funamori Yasaburo Moto Gosho" (*Gosho Zenshu*, pp. 1445–46), written in June 1261 when the Daishonin was 40. Editor's note: The Gosho text here may differ in places from what appears in the *Major Writings* or other previously published translations. This is so that the wording of the English text will accord more smoothly with the modern Japanese translation of the original Japanese Gosho. (The author is using a modern Japanese rendering of the classical Japanese original as the basis of his lectures in this series.)

2. At Kawana, a fishing village on the northeastern coast of Izu Peninsula.

3. Soka Kyoiku Gakkai (Society for Value-Creating Education), predecessor of the Soka Gakkai.

4. From the essay "History and Conviction of the Soka Gakkai."

'The Izu Exile' (2)

But I would like to mention one thing in particular. When the steward of this district requested that I pray for his recovery from illness, I wondered if I should accept it. But since he showed me some degree of faith in [the Lotus Sutra], I decided I would appeal to the Lotus Sutra. If I did, I saw no reason why the ten demon daughters should not join forces to aid me. I therefore addressed the Lotus Sutra, Shakyamuni, Taho and the other Buddhas of the ten directions, the Sun Goddess, Hachiman and the other heavenly and earthly deities, both major and minor. I was sure that they would consider my request and respond by producing a sign of his recovery. Certainly they would never forsake me, but would respond as attentively as a person rubs a sore or scratches an itch. And as it turned out, the steward recovered. In gratitude he presented me with a statue of the Buddha which had appeared from the sea along with a catch of fish. This was on account of his illness — an illness which I am certain was inflicted by the ten demon daughters. This benefit will certainly pass on to you and your wife. (MW-2 [2ND ED.], 55)[1]

Manifesting the Entity of the Buddha in Our Lives

How can I help everyone become happy?" "How can I enable everyone to receive great benefit?" This is the Buddha's constant thought.

Nichiren Daishonin says that the benefit that he has received will assuredly become the benefit of Funamori Yasaburo and his wife. The benefit that votaries of the Lotus Sutra gain through their activities is shared by those who support them. The great benefit of the SGI in advancing the worldwide propagation of the Mystic Law is in its entirety the SGI members' good fortune and benefit.

A little more than a month after the Daishonin was exiled to Izu, Ito Hachiro Zaemon, the steward of the district, fell gravely ill. His symptoms were so severe that the Daishonin says, "It appeared that he would certainly die" (*Gosho Zenshu*, p. 1225).

All the power and influence in the world cannot cure illness, or even extend one's life for an hour. Wealth, status and worldly power essentially count for nothing in the face of the fundamental sufferings in life: birth, aging, sickness and death. To Nichiren Daishonin, the steward was a human being like anyone else; his sufferings were no different from the sufferings of all living beings.

But if the afflicted person does not believe in the Mystic Law, then even the prayers of the Buddha will not accomplish anything. Buddhism is reason. Because the steward had evinced a degree of faith, the Daishonin, with his immense compassion, could cure his illness.

The steward, having escaped death, greatly appreciated the Daishonin's concern for him and presented him with a wooden statue of Shakyamuni that a fisherman had found at sea.

This was a time when faith in Amida Buddha and other creeds was widespread, and initially the Daishonin's call had been to return to the prime point of Shakyamuni. It was no doubt that with that spirit he accepted the statue — not as an object of worship. Also, it is possible that, as the original Buddha, he may have had a kind of fondness for the statue of Shakyamuni, as if for a child.

The Daishonin says that his benefit as the votary of the Lotus Sutra will pass on to Yasaburo and his wife. The Buddha's constant prayer is to share his benefit with all others.

When the Daishonin was taken from Kamakura to the execution grounds at Tatsunokuchi, he remarked to Shijo Kingo, who had rushed to his side, "Now I will present my severed head to the Lotus Sutra and share the blessings therefrom with my parents, and with my disciples and believers" (MW-1, 181). This is the spirit of the original Buddha.

By contrast, there are those, like the members of the Nichiren Shoshu priesthood today, who are under the illusion that they are absolute, who arrogantly suppose themselves to be different from and better than others. In light of the Gosho, such people definitely are not practicing the Daishonin's Buddhism.

We, living beings, have dwelt in the sea of the sufferings of birth and death since time without beginning. But now that we have become votaries of the Lotus Sutra, we will without fail attain the Buddha's entity which is as indestructible as a diamond, realizing that our bodies and minds that have existed since the beginningless past are inherently endowed with the eternally unchanging nature, and thus awakening to our mystic reality with our mystic wisdom. Then how can we be in any way different from the Buddha? Shakyamuni Buddha, the lord of teachings, who declared in the remote past of *gohyaku-jintengo*, "I am the only person who can rescue and protect others" (LS3, 70), is none other than each of us, living beings. This is the Lotus Sutra's doctrine of the three thousand realms in a single moment of life, and the conducts of the Buddha who says "I am always here, preaching the Law" (LS16, 229). How valuable, then, are the Lotus Sutra and Shakyamuni Buddha for us, but we, ordinary people, are never aware of it. This is the meaning of the passage in the *Juryo* chapter, "[I am always here, but through my transcendental power] I make it so that living beings in their befuddlement do not see me even when close by" (LS16, 229). The difference between delusion and enlightenment is like the four different views of the grove of sal trees.[2] Let it be known that the Buddha with the three thousand realms in a single moment of life is any living being

> in any of the realms of existence who manifests his
> inherent Buddhahood. (MW-2 [2ND ED.], 55–56)

I think we can interpret this as Nichiren Daishonin's human rights declaration.

People drifting in a sea of suffering, like the statue of the Buddha that appeared from the sea, are in fact entities of the Buddha. We ourselves are the Shakyamuni Buddha who attained enlightenment in the remote past. A true practitioner of the Lotus Sutra remembers this. The Daishonin says that through the practice of the Mystic Law, we can definitely attain "the Buddha's entity which is as indestructible as a diamond."

We can attain a happy life state that shines like a diamond, solemn and indestructible under all circumstances. And we can do so in this lifetime. The Lotus Sutra exists to enable all people to attain such a state.

The "Buddha who is a common mortal" specifically refers to the Daishonin. But in a general sense, it also indicates the followers of the Daishonin who are one with him in spirit. And the "Lotus Sutra's doctrine of the three thousand realms in a single moment of life" is the teaching proclaiming that all people are Buddhas.

Specifically, it is the Gohonzon — the actual embodiment of this principle that a life-moment possesses three thousand realms — that enables all people to become Buddhas. When we actively base our lives on the Gohonzon, wisdom and vitality well forth, and we enter a rhythm of total and complete victory.

Since the Gohonzon is "always here, preaching the Law," by chanting daimoku we can, under any circumstances, gain the wisdom to know the proper course of action. The Daishonin says, "When the skies are clear, the ground is illuminated" (MW-1, 82). Similarly, when the sun of wisdom rises in our lives, the correct path becomes apparent.

"Living beings in their befuddlement" means people who, failing to grasp this, suppose the Buddha or Shakyamuni to be a remote, abstract being.

> The demon who appeared before Sessen Doji[3] was Taishaku in disguise. The dove which sought the protection of King Shibi was the god Bishukatsuma.[4] King Fumyo,[5] who returned to the castle of King Hansoku, was Shakyamuni Buddha, the lord of teachings. The eyes of common mortals cannot see their true identities, but the eyes of the Buddha can. As the sutra states, the sky and the sea both have paths for birds and fish to come and go. A wooden statue [of the Buddha] is itself a golden Buddha, and a golden Buddha is a wooden statue. Aniruddha's[6] gold was seen first as a hare and then as a corpse. Sand in the palm of Mahanama's[7] hand turned into gold. These things are beyond ordinary understanding. [Similarly] a common mortal is a Buddha, and a Buddha a common mortal. This is exactly what is meant by the doctrine of the three thousand realms in a single moment of life and by the phrase, "I in fact attained Buddhahood" (LS16,

225) [which declares that the common mortal is the Buddha of the *Juryo* chapter].

Thus it is quite possible that you and your wife have appeared here as reincarnations of the World-Honored One of Great Enlightenment [Shakyamuni], the lord of teachings, in order to help me. (MW-2 [2ND ED.], 56–57)

When we change our state of life, our view of everything alters. Seen with the eyes of common mortals, a common mortal appears simply as a common mortal; but seen with the eyes of the Buddha, ordinary people, just as they are, are Buddhas. Yasaburo and his wife appeared to the Daishonin's enlightened eyes as reincarnations of Shakyamuni, the lord of teachings.

In contrast to the present age, in the Daishonin's day people who hunted or fished for a living were accorded low social status. The Daishonin regards Yasaburo and his wife, who were involved in such work, as Buddhas. He applauds and reveres them with palms together. By the common sense of thirteenth-century Japan, this would have been unthinkable.

A Buddha holds others in the highest regard; the ability to do so is the Buddha's intrinsic virtue. Kosen-rufu means promulgating this attitude of respect for human beings.

When the Daishonin wrote this letter, he was an alleged criminal. Socially, he was in the absolute worst situation. Nonetheless, he based himself on the highest state of life.

By contrast, the authorities who persecuted the Daishonin, and the evil priests in league with them, may well have thought themselves to occupy the high ground. But these were people who, "despising and looking down on all humankind" (LS13, 193), in fact inhabited the lowest and most pitiful state of life.

> Although the distance between Ito and Kawana is short, we are not allowed to communicate openly. I am writing this letter for your future reference. Do not discuss these matters with other people, but ponder them yourselves. If anyone should learn anything at all about this letter, it will go hard with you. Keep this deep in your heart, and never speak about it. With my deepest regard. Nam-myoho-renge-kyo.
>
> Nichiren
>
> The twenty-seventh day of the sixth month in the first year of Kocho (1261)
>
> To be sent to Funamori Yasaburo (MW-2 [2ND ED.], 57)

In concluding the letter, the Daishonin shows great concern for his followers' situation. Ito is only a short distance from Kawana. But under the circumstances, the Daishonin could not encourage them directly — even sending a letter was dangerous. The Daishonin's situation was as severe as ever, so he may have had Yasaburo's messenger wait while he hastily composed this response.

From start to finish, every line of the letter exudes the Daishonin's sense of gratitude to Yasaburo and his wife. He praises them highly, saying that they are surely votaries of the Lotus Sutra. He compares them to his own mother and father, Buddhist gods, and reincarnations of Shakyamuni, the lord of teachings.

Since it might put them in danger if it became known that they had even received a letter from the Daishonin, he tells them, "Keep this deep in your heart," so great was his concern.

It is a very heartfelt letter. The Daishonin's warm character drew people to him. There were probably disciples who were attracted to the Daishonin by the depth of his thought or philosophy, and others who approached his Buddhist teaching for transforming destiny out of their sense of desperation, as though grasping at straws. But what most drew people to the Daishonin was no doubt his profound humanity.

The people who hated and envied the Daishonin could not understand this. To those who look down on others, even actions of the greatest sincerity, undertaken out of respect for others, appear distorted. The state of the world today is such that egoism is taken for granted. In such an environment, we struggle to spread the correct Buddhist teaching and to encourage others. We carry out the work of Buddhas and bodhisattvas.

In light of this Gosho, we are all entities of the Buddha "as indestructible as diamonds." With great sincerity we look after and encourage friends, as though embracing them with our very lives. Through such continued action, we solidify the entity of the Buddha in our lives.

Walt Whitman sings, "Henceforth I ask not good-fortune, I myself am good-fortune...."[8]

Good fortune does not lie far away. Our lives themselves are entities of good fortune, entities of happiness as indestructible as diamonds. That's what this Gosho resoundingly proclaims.

1. "Funamori Yasaburo moto gosho" (*Gosho Zenshu*, pp. 1445–46), written in June 1261 when the Daishonin was 40. Editor's note: The Gosho text here may differ in places from what appears in the *Major Writings* or other previously published translations. This is so that the wording of the English text will accord more smoothly with the modern Japanese translation of the original Japanese Gosho. (The author is using a modern Japanese rendering of the classical Japanese original as the basis of his lectures in this series.)

2. The grove of sal trees where Shakyamuni expounded his last teaching, the Nirvana Sutra, and passed away. The Zobo Ketsugi Sutra defines the grove of sal trees in four different ways, according to the capacities and life states of common mortals, people of the two vehicles, bodhisattvas and the Buddha.

3. The name of Shakyamuni in a previous lifetime. To test Sessen Doji's seeking spirit, the god Taishaku appeared before him in the form of a hungry demon.

4. When Shakyamuni in a past existence practiced austerities as King Shibi, Taishaku, to test his sincerity, assumed the

form of a hawk, and Bishukatsuma, who serves Taishaku, that of a dove. To save the dove, Shibi gave his life, offering his flesh to the hungry hawk.

5. King Fumyo was Shakyamuni's name when he was engaged in the practice of observing the precepts in a previous existence. Captured by King Hansoku, Fumyo was about to be executed. Lamenting that he had promised offerings to a certain monk, but now would have to break his promise, he received a grace period of seven days. Fumyo thereupon returned to his country, gave the offerings to the monk, and transferred the throne to his son. After proclaiming that keeping promises is the most important precept, he returned to his captor. Hansoku was so impressed by Fumyo's sincerity that he released him and converted to Buddhism.

6. Aniruddha was one of Shakyamuni's ten major disciples, known as the foremost in divine insight. The story referred to is found in the *Hokke Mongu*.

7. Mahanama was one of the five monks ordered by Shakyamuni's father, the king, to accompany Shakyamuni when he forsook the secular world and entered religious life. According to the Zoichi-agon Sutra, Mahanama is said to have possessed occult powers. The story of "sand in his palm turning into gold" is found in Ts'ung-i's *Tendai sandaibu hochu*.

8. Walt Whitman, "Song of the Open Road," *Leaves of Grass* (New York: Everyman's Library, 1968), p. 125.

'The Opening of the Eyes' (1)

Spiritual Victory in the Midst of a Great Storm

A totally cloudless sky. An endless sea of blue. My mentor, Josei Toda, once used these images to describe Nichiren Daishonin's life state while in exile on Sado Island:

> If it were people like us [who were in exile on Sado], our lives would be in the depths of hell itself. But in the case of Nichiren Daishonin, who was utterly invincible and free from fear, we find that his life from moment to moment was as [vast and serene as] the ocean or the sky.

In "The Opening of the Eyes,"[1] the Daishonin says: "I, Nichiren, am the richest man in all of present-day Japan. I have dedicated my life to the Lotus Sutra, and my name will be handed down in ages to come" (MW-2 [2ND ED.], 151).

In the Daishonin's day, the winters on Sado were a great deal more severe than they are today. And he was living at Tsukahara in a dilapidated shrine called Sanmai-do. Socially, he was an exile. His life was constantly in jeopardy. Under such conditions, with the roar of a lion, he voiced this declaration as a king of the spirit.

Arriving at Tsukahara on November 1, 1271, Nichiren Daishonin began composing lengthy manuscripts with an awesome vigor; the image that comes to my mind is that of a great waterfall. In the second month of the following year, he entrusted a messenger from Shijo Kingo with a Gosho intended for all of his followers—"The Opening of the Eyes."

Even amid the blowing snows on Sado, his conviction in the justice of his actions was like a flame. It definitely was not extinguished; rather, his burning spirit to lead all people to happiness blazed all the more brilliantly.

With this writing, he wanted to convey his immense life state to his followers, to show them that only through waging a great life-or-death struggle can one manifest a truly immense state of life. He wanted to establish this truth for all time.

While the original manuscript of "The Opening of the Eyes" is not extant, it is said to have been sixty-six pages long, with sixty-five pages of text and a cover page reading "Opening of the Eyes."

The title refers to opening the eyes, or the minds, of the Japanese people. In light of the sutras, it is clear that Nichiren Daishonin was truly a person of justice. With this writing, the Daishonin declares that he is the votary of the Lotus Sutra and, hence, the Buddha of the Latter Day of the Law.

LEARNING FROM THE GOSHO • 51

I hope that, by studying the final section of this writing, we can learn about the Daishonin's towering state of life.

> Question: When you condemn the evil of the followers of the Nembutsu and Zen sects and arouse their enmity, what merit does that bring?
>
> Answer: The Nirvana Sutra says, "If even a good monk sees someone destroying the teaching and disregards him, failing to reproach him, to oust him or to bring his offense to light, then you should realize that that monk is an enemy of Buddhism from within. But if he ousts the destroyer of the Law, reproaches him or exposes his offense, then he is my [the Buddha's] disciple and a true voice-hearer."
>
> Chang-an comments on this as follows: "One who destroys or brings confusion to the Buddha's teachings is an enemy of Buddhism from within. If one befriends another person but lacks the mercy to correct him, one is in fact his enemy. But one who reprimands and corrects an offender is a voice-hearer who defends the Buddha's teachings, a true disciple of the Buddha. One who rids the offender of evil is acting as his parent. Those who reproach offenders are disciples of the Buddha. But those who do not oust offenders are enemies of Buddhism from within."[2] (MW-2 [2ND ED.], 186)

It is one thing if a person does something wrong, but all too often those doing good are vilified and attacked. While completely unreasonable, this is the reality of society.

The great author Leo Tolstoy said: "You cannot live without enemies.... And the fact of the matter is, the more upright you live, the more enemies you will have."[3]

Never has anyone called out for justice as did the Daishonin. Never has anyone fought so hard for the happiness of all people. As a result, he encountered one persecution after another. And, in what was tantamount to a death sentence, he was exiled to Sado Island.

The persecution was directed against his followers, too. Some were imprisoned, others had fiefs taken away and still others were banished. The confusion and unrest among the Daishonin's followers was intense. Fearful, many discarded their faith or simply fell silent.

Some disciples even, with knowing looks on their faces, criticized their mentor, telling people things like, "If you are more flexible in spreading the teaching, you won't face persecutions like those besetting our revered teacher."

At the end of "The Opening of the Eyes," Nichiren Daishonin addresses this. He poses the question: In propagating this teaching, what merit does it bring, what can you gain, if you arouse the enmity of those around you? Citing a sutra passage, the Daishonin replies: Doesn't the Nirvana Sutra say that those seeking to destroy the Law should be reproached and driven away, that their offenses be made clear, that they cannot be simply disregarded? Doesn't it say that people should be reproached for their evil, ousted and their offenses brought to light?

In essence, treating someone who tries to subvert the teachings in this manner is a practice of compassion necessary to protect Buddhism. Therefore, although those who carry this out may encounter persecution, they can definitely attain Buddhahood. And, the Daishonin says, there is no greater merit or benefit than this.

"My disciples," he cries, "do not be afraid!" "Live with pride and dignity, chests out and heads held high, like lion kings!" Out of his immense compassion, he wishes to convey to all his disciples his desire for them to lead good lives and continue advancing along the path of belief that they have resolved to follow.

Buddhism only exists in action. Through action, the Mystic Law inherent in our lives begins to shine. The Buddhist gods and all Buddhas protect people of action; those who consistently take action for justice are truly happy.

Nichiren Daishonin was stronger than anyone. And what was the source of his strength? It was his concern for the people.

But it seems that the Daishonin's strength was generally misunderstood. Toward Hei no Saemon and wicked priests, the Daishonin was the severest foe. Yet he teaches his followers that in spreading the teaching to others, they should conduct themselves courteously. For example, he advised one person to always speak "mildly but firmly in a quiet voice with a calm gaze and an even expression" (MW-4, 122).

Again, in his landmark treatise the "Rissho Ankoku Ron," which takes the form of a dialogue between a traveler and a host, the host (representing the Daishonin) never at any point raises his voice. On the contrary, when the guest becomes agitated, the host soothes him, smiles brightly and tenaciously continues the dialogue. We can take it that the Daishonin depicts the host in such a way because this was how he himself conducted dialogue.

> If we examine the *Hoto* chapter of the Lotus Sutra, we find Shakyamuni Buddha, Taho Buddha and the various Buddhas from the ten directions who are emanations of Shakyamuni Buddha gathering together. And why? As the sutra itself says, "Each...has come to this place on purpose to make certain the Law will long endure" (LS11, 177). Shakyamuni, Taho and the other Buddhas intend to insure the future propagation of the Lotus Sutra so that it can be made available to every single living being, the children of the Buddha, in times to come. We may surmise from this that their concern and compassion are even greater than that of a father and mother who see their only child inflicted with great suffering. Honen, however, indifferent to their pain, would tightly shut the gates to the Lotus Sutra in the Latter Day of the Law so that no one would have access to it. Like a person who tricks a demented child into throwing away his treasure, he induces people to discard the Lotus Sutra, a shameless thing to do indeed!

> If someone is about to kill your father and mother, shouldn't you try to warn them? If a bad son who

is insane with drink is threatening to kill his father and mother, shouldn't you try to stop him? If some evil person is about to set fire to the temples and pagodas, shouldn't you try to stop him? If your only child is gravely ill, shouldn't you try to cure him with moxibustion treatment? To fail to do so is to act like those people who see but do not try to put a stop to the Zen and Nembutsu followers in Japan. As Chang-an says, "If one befriends another person but lacks the mercy to correct him, one is in fact his enemy." (MW-2 [2ND ED.], 186–87)

The Buddha Yearns To Save Those Most Miserable

With what intention do Shakyamuni, Taho and Shakyamuni's emanations, the Buddhas of the ten directions, gather in one place in "Emergence of the Treasure Tower" (Hoto), the eleventh chapter of the Lotus Sutra? They do so entirely out of their desire to ensure the future propagation of the Lotus Sutra, to see to it that the Lotus Sutra is made available to all living beings, who are all children of the Buddha, in the future.

The Nirvana Sutra relates that just before Shakyamuni died, he lamented: "I will shortly die. The matter of King Ajatashatru is my only misgiving."

King Ajatashatru was for many years bitterly hostile toward Shakyamuni, and even tried to kill him. He had murdered his own father, the king, to take over the throne.

But even as king, inwardly his life was impoverished and empty. Shakyamuni was deeply pained by the thought of Ajatashatru's unhappiness.

A disciple then asked Shakyamuni, "If the Buddha's compassion is directed toward all beings equally, then why are you concerned only about King Ajatashatru?"

Shakyamuni answered: "Consider the case of a couple that has seven children. The parents love all their children equally and without discrimination. But if one child falls ill, won't the parents be most concerned about that sick child?

"I will definitely not abandon — I will not forget — the person who is the most miserable. Rather, I will try hardest of all to save that person." This is the Buddha's conviction.

Nichiren Daishonin strove to save all the people of Japan, including those who had persecuted him and even exiled him to Sado.

President Toda said, "Because of the Daishonin's love for the people of Japan, he directly accepted the onslaught of the three powerful enemies, thinking nothing of the great persecutions that befell him time and again." The Daishonin, while on Sado, goes so far as to say, "I pray that before anything else I can guide to the truth the sovereign and those others who persecuted me" (MW-1, 117).

What a magnanimity of spirit!

From the time he declared the establishment of his teaching, the Daishonin never retreated a step in his great and merciful struggle for the people, whom he loved as his own children. In "The Opening of the Eyes," the Daishonin indicates his frame of mind prior to establishing his teaching on

April 28, 1253, saying he was fully aware that if he did not speak out and proclaim the correct Buddhist teaching for the Latter Day, he "would be lacking in compassion" (MW-1, 95).

To spread this Buddhism would mean encountering great obstacles. Had he not spoken out, he could well have led a peaceful and secure existence — but to have done so, he says, would have been lacking in compassion.

No matter how compassionate some might appear, if they fail to take action it is the same as if they have no compassion; they lack compassion.

The opposite of compassion is "false friendship" — falsely befriending another. This term clearly mirrors the state of society today. President Toda proclaimed: "People's lives today lack any sense of compassion.... Isn't a lack of compassion the prime characteristic of the present age?"

Society today is very cruel and unforgiving. In this compassionless society, SGI members are working to relieve people of their sufferings and impart true joy, while proclaiming the truth from the very depths of their lives out of genuine concern for others.

Through our efforts at dialogue, through our actions, we are fundamentally changing a society that lacks compassion and is awash with false friendship. We are transforming the destiny of our society, which has a tendency to be discriminatory and lacking in compassion. We are sending the sunlight of spring to a society that is locked in a frigid winter. We are thawing people's hearts with a warm current of humanity.

I am confident that, without a doubt, the Daishonin most highly praises all of you who are steadfastly carrying through with the bodhisattva practice of compassion as true disciples and as "followers who share my spirit."

1. "The Opening of the Eyes" (*Gosho Zenshu*, pp. 186–237; MW-2, 59–188), written in February 1272 when the Daishonin was 51. Editor's Note: The Gosho text here may differ in places from what appears in the *Major Writings* or other previously published translations. This is so that the wording of the English text will accord more smoothly with the modern Japanese translation of the original Japanese Gosho. (The author is using a modern Japanese rendering of the classical Japanese original as the basis of his lectures in this series.)

2. "Nehangyo Sho."

3. Translated from the Japanese: Leo Tolstoy, *Torusutoi nikkisho* (Diaries of Leo Tolstoy), trans. Yoshitaro Yosemura (Tokyo: Iwanami Shoten, 1935), p. 112.

'The Opening of the Eyes' (2)

Justice is like the sun. A society that lacks justice is as though shrouded in darkness. No one can stop the sun from rising. No cloud can hide the rays of the sun indefinitely. "Opening the eyes" means causing those whose hearts are steeped in darkness to recognize the existence of the sun of justice.

> I, Nichiren, am sovereign, teacher, father and mother to all the people of Japan. But the men of the Tendai sect [who do not refute the misleading sects] are all great enemies of the people. As Chang-an has noted,[1] "One who rids the offender of evil is acting as his parent."

> One who has not set one's mind upon the way can never free oneself from the sufferings of birth and death. (MW-2 [2ND ED.], 187)

The Buddha Illuminates the World
With the Three Virtues

Nichiren Daishonin says that he is "sovereign, teacher, father and mother to all the people of Japan." The three virtues — sovereign, teacher and parent — indicate the state of life, brilliant as the sun, of a true person of justice.

A passage of the Gosho "Repaying Debts of Gratitude" comes immediately to mind:

> If Nichiren's compassion is truly great and encompassing, Nam-myoho-renge-kyo will spread for ten thousand years and more, for all eternity, for it has the beneficial power to open the blind eyes of every living being in the country of Japan, and it blocks off the road that leads to the hell of incessant suffering. (MW-4, 272)

High Priest Nichikan interprets this passage as referring to the Daishonin's three virtues. "If Nichiren's compassion is truly great and encompassing, Nam-myoho-renge-kyo will spread for ten thousand years and more, for all eternity" indicates his immense compassion, or virtue as the parent. "It has the beneficial power to open the blind eyes of every living being in the country of Japan" indicates the power to open people's minds or inner eyes, i.e., the teacher. And, "it blocks off the road that leads to the hell of incessant suffering" indicates the sovereign who struggles to ensure that the people do not slip into misery.[2]

"The Opening of the Eyes" begins: "There are three categories of people that all human beings should respect. They are the sovereign, the teacher and the parent" (MW-2 [2ND ED.], 59). The purpose of this writing is to clarify the true virtues of the sovereign, the teacher and the parent. Nichiren Daishonin perfectly possesses all three.

In a general sense, the sovereign, teacher and parent might be thought of — to put it in modern terms — as the three necessary attributes of leaders. The virtue of the sovereign lies in protecting people; this corresponds to an unwavering sense of responsibility. The virtue of the teacher lies in guiding people; this is the shining wisdom to guide people along the path of happiness. And the virtue of the parent lies in lovingly raising people; this is a warm, if strict, compassion.

A sense of responsibility, wisdom and compassion — are not these the most important qualities for leaders, and for all people, to possess? If even a few more leaders possessed these three attributes, it would contribute immensely to easing tension and the general happiness of humankind. But the fact of the matter is that the tendency of all too many leaders in society is just the opposite.

The antithesis of the virtue of the sovereign is irresponsibility. We have leaders who carry on in a self-aggrandizing and high-handed manner, but who avoid addressing difficult issues, using the rationale that "someone else will take care of it," or that "things will somehow work themselves out." They order other people around, and then try to shirk responsibility. Even though they may have the appearance of leaders, they do not qualify as such. They lack the requisite virtue.

The "Life Span" chapter of the Lotus Sutra explains the three virtues of the essential teaching. "This, my land, remains safe and tranquil" (LS16, 230) indicates the virtue of the sovereign who works resolutely to ensure the peace and tranquillity of the land or community for which he or she is responsible.

"Constantly I have preached the Law, teaching, converting" (LS16, 229) indicates the virtue of the teacher. As indicated by the word *constantly*, meaning "without rest or interruption," a teacher unstintingly uses his or her voice to help others.

The virtue of the parent is indicated by the line, "I am the father of this world" (LS16, 231). The parent loves people because they are children of the Buddha who will one day become Buddhas, and takes action on their behalf.

Leaders also must have the ability to provide training, protection, guidance and instruction. When someone has a problem, they need to provide kind guidance as well as necessary instruction. By so doing, they can ensure that people do not become deadlocked.

A genuine leader protects people when they are tired, and nurtures them by providing training appropriate to their levels of development. If people are given strict training under circumstances that require protection instead, they will go under. And if they are protectively coddled when instead they need guidance, they will stop growing.

If we relate these desirable leadership attributes to the three virtues, the ability to protect corresponds to the virtue of the sovereign, the ability to provide guidance and instruction to the virtue of the teacher, and the ability to provide training to the virtue of the parent. The determination, prayer and strength to help people become happy are the keys to outstanding leadership.

In connection with the characterization in "Repaying Debts of Gratitude" of the virtue of the sovereign as "blocking off the road that leads to the hell of incessant suffering," High Priest Nichikan asks, "How could the opening or closing of roads be left up to a retainer? [Matters of such importance must be attended to by the sovereign.]" The virtue of the sovereign lies in closing off paths of evil and opening up paths of good.

"I want to close off the path leading to Hell." This was the spirit with which Josei Toda declared his opposition to the use of nuclear weapons: "Anyone who threatens the right to live is a devil, a Satan and a monster."[3] To resolutely close off the path to war and open up the path to peace — this is the virtue of the sovereign, and the responsibility of leaders.

The SGI, as the true inheritor of Nichiren Daishonin's Buddhism, has opened a path of peace spanning the globe. Twenty years ago, when China and the Soviet Union were in conflict and the Americans and the Soviets were mired in the Cold War, who could have imagined the state of the world today? The Soka Gakkai, despite storms of criticism, has bravely taken action to close off the path to confrontation and open the path to friendship.

"There must never be World War III!" We have prayed and taken action with a sense of responsibility to see that such a calamity never comes to pass. Toward that end, we have developed a movement of peace, culture and education based on Buddhism.

Broadly speaking, creating a land of peace and tranquillity — as in the passage, "This, my land, remains safe and tranquil" —

indicates the virtue of the sovereign. Education represents the virtue of the teacher. And culture, because it fosters people's inner lives, relates to the virtue of the parent. We are extending this path of the three virtues throughout the entire world.

Once a path is opened, those who come after can travel along it with composure and ease. Nichiren Daishonin, as the Buddha of the Latter Day possessing the virtues of sovereign, teacher and parent, opened a path to the enlightenment of all people. For this we owe him our eternal gratitude.

To extend and expand the path that the mentor has graciously opened is the mission of disciples. And the path that the Daishonin opened now spans the entire world. Through the struggles of our fellow members — the wondrous Bodhisattvas of the Earth — the great path of happiness now runs through 128 countries. The sun of justice has begun to rise. I am absolutely convinced that the original Buddha, Nichiren Daishonin, accords the highest praise to those who dedicate themselves to this noble task.

In the Gosho passage we will study next, the Daishonin says that the followers of the Tendai school are great enemies of the people. While aware that the Lotus Sutra is the foremost teaching, they not only failed to combat evil but took the side of those persecuting the Daishonin.

Tsunesaburo Makiguchi said, "Of all the Nichiren schools existing today, Nichiren Shoshu, it would seem, most closely resembles the Tendai school of the Daishonin's time."[4]

He was exactly right. The members of the Nichiren Shoshu priesthood, who have repeatedly obstructed kosen-rufu, a sacred undertaking for the people's happiness, are indeed great enemies of the people. History has now shown the concordance of their actions with the Daishonin's assertion in "The Opening of the Eyes."

Encountering Great Persecution Is the Highest Honor

Shakyamuni Buddha, the lord of teachings, was cursed by all the followers of non-Buddhist teachings and labeled as a man of great evil. The Great Teacher T'ien-t'ai was regarded with intense enmity by the three schools of the south and seven schools of the north, and Tokuitsu of Japan criticized him for using his three-inch tongue to try to denounce Shakyamuni's teachings and destroy the five-foot body of the Buddha.[5] The Great Teacher Dengyo was disparaged by the monks of Nara, who said, "Saicho[6] has never been to the capital of T'ang China!" But all of these abuses were incurred because of the Lotus Sutra, and they are therefore no shame to the men who suffered them. To be praised by fools — that is the greatest shame. Now that I have incurred the wrath of the authorities [and am now in exile], the priests of the Tendai and Shingon sects are no doubt delighted. They are strange and shameless men. (MW-2 [2ND ED.], 187–8)

Justice is certain to meet with persecution, just as the sun is sure to be obstructed by clouds. Difficulties are the proof of justice. Encountering great persecution is the highest honor.

Even Shakyamuni was derided as a "person of great evil." The Great Teacher T'ien-t'ai was showered with abuse by the ten powerful schools of his day. And he was still being vilified 200 years later. The priest Tokuichi of Japan's Hosso school went so far as to say: "What a foolish thing you have done, Chiko (T'ien-t'ai). You have slandered Shakyamuni's lifetime teaching and brought confusion to the world."

The Great Teacher Dengyo was reviled by the schools of Nara. They said, "While Saicho says that he went to China, he quickly came back without having visited the capital after only studying a short time in the provinces."

T'ien-t'ai and Dengyo received such criticism because they advocated the Lotus Sutra, because they issued the call to return to the spirit of the Lotus Sutra, of Shakyamuni. Those who do not take action will face neither criticism nor slander.

On the other hand, those who thought they were only criticizing T'ien-t'ai and Dengyo were in fact trampling on the spirit of Shakyamuni. The more such individuals slander the sutra's votaries, the more they are in effect slandering the Lotus Sutra. Moreover, such individuals entirely fail to realize this. No one is more foolish or pitiful.

Those who delighted when the Daishonin — a person of justice whose actions exactly matched with the Lotus Sutra — was sent into exile and the correct teaching was attacked were the true fools.

"To be praised by fools — that is the greatest shame." President Makiguchi made this his motto. He was persecuted by the military powers and betrayed by the Nichiren Shoshu priesthood. Yet he laughed this off.

Lecturing on "The Opening of the Eyes," President Josei Toda said:

> Based on these words, Mr. Makiguchi did not regard it as shameful to undergo criticism or persecution for the Lotus Sutra. He died in prison for his beliefs because he propagated Nam-myoho-renge-kyo of the Three Great Secret Laws, the essence of the Lotus Sutra, based on the conviction that to be praised by fools is the greatest disgrace and to be praised by the great sage [Nichiren Daishonin] is the greatest glory. I believe that he provides the foremost model for all who embrace faith in the Buddhism of Nichiren Daishonin.[7]

And he cried out to youth:

> In the struggle for the Law in the polluted Latter Day, your desire should be to win the Daishonin's praise as brilliant young warriors. For a person of wisdom, to be praised by fools is the greatest disgrace. To be praised by the great sage is the greatest honor in life.[8]

These words, which presidents Makiguchi and Toda both made their motto are also the Soka Gakkai motto. To put this golden motto into practice is the eternal spirit of the Gakkai.

Let us in the SGI advance in a manner befitting the SGI! Let us proceed straight ahead along this path, along the glorious path of Soka! If people want to laugh, let them laugh. If people want to vilify us, let them go right ahead.

Can such individuals reveal a means for others to become happy? Can listening to what they have to say bring people relief from suffering? No, definitely not.

The Soka Gakkai is a lion — completely fearless. It is enough that we conduct ourselves in such a manner that we win the praise of the original Buddha, Nichiren Daishonin. Future generations will definitely celebrate our efforts.

Even As an Exile, the Daishonin Felt Immense Joy

Shakyamuni Buddha appeared in the *saha* world, Kumarajiva journeyed to the Ch'in dynasty in China,[9] and Dengyo likewise went to China [all for the sake of the Lotus Sutra]. Aryadeva and Aryasimha sacrificed their bodies. Bodhisattva Yakuo burned his arms as an offering, and Prince Shotoku stripped off the skin on his hand [and copied the sutra on it].[10] Shakyamuni, when he was a bodhisattva, sold his flesh to make offerings, and another time, when he was a bodhisattva named Gyobo, he used his bone as a pen [to write down the Buddha's teaching].

T'ien-t'ai has said that "the method chosen should be that which accords with the time." The propagation of the Buddhist teachings should follow the time. For what I have done, I have been condemned

> to exile, but it is a small suffering to undergo in this
> present life and not one worth lamenting. In future
> lives I will enjoy immense happiness, a thought that
> gives me great joy. (MW-2 [2ND ED.], 188)

Shakyamuni chose to be born in the *saha* world, a world fraught with suffering, to expound the Lotus Sutra. To translate the Lotus Sutra, Kumarajiva traveled from Central Asia to China, undergoing many hardships along the way. And in pursuit of the essence of the Lotus Sutra, the Great Teacher Dengyo made the journey over treacherous seas from Japan to China.

In each case, a great sense of purpose produced action. An irrepressible spirit gives rise to action.

Bodhisattva Aryadeva and the worthy Aryasimha, who inherited Shakyamuni's teaching, admonished evil rulers and laid down their lives for the teaching. It is also related that Bodhisattva Medicine King (Yakuo) burned his elbows as an offering to the Buddha, and that Prince Shotoku of Japan peeled the skin off his hand for use as paper on which to copy the titles of sutras.

In a previous existence when Shakyamuni, as a bodhisattva, was practicing to attain enlightenment, he once sold his own flesh to make an offering to the Buddha. Another time, as Gyobo Bonji, he is said to have used his skin as paper, his bone as a pen and his blood as ink in order to copy down the Buddha's teaching.

The form that Buddhist practice takes differs according to the time. Buddhism "accords with the time," but the fundamental path and spirit do not change. The main point is to wholeheartedly dedicate oneself to the Law and to people's happiness.

The True Law has been handed down thanks to the painstaking efforts of such people. It has been conveyed through a relay of individuals who have each taken action according with the time in which they have lived. This is itself a great achievement in Buddhist history.

But Nichiren Daishonin says that those who spread the Mystic Law in the Latter Day are far nobler than even these practitioners of the Former and Middle Days of the Law. All of you are courageous and noble people of mission opening a path where none has before existed, spreading the Daishonin's Buddhism amid storms of obstacles and calumny. The Daishonin cannot but praise you. Let us be confident that Shakyamuni, Many Treasures (Taho) Buddha and all Buddhas of the ten directions also greatly extol our efforts to spread the Mystic Law in a manner that accords with the Latter Day.

The Daishonin concludes "The Opening of the Eyes" on an exultant note: "For what I have done, I have been condemned to exile, but it is a small suffering to undergo in this present life and not one worth lamenting. In future lives I will enjoy immense happiness, a thought that gives me great joy." This is his great declaration of a spiritual victory that shines in human history.

The Daishonin was an exile, completely without freedom. He was confined to the tiny island of Sado, a kind of natural prison. President Toda once said, "In modern terms, exile to Sado is comparable to being banished to the Sahara Desert." And yet, the Daishonin's spirit was that of a king. No one could put his heart in chains. No sword of persecution could make the slightest nick in his spirit.

From the vantage point of the sun of *kuon ganjo*, as from high above, he surveyed with perfect composure even the most violent storms of persecution. The pride and conviction to thoroughly dedicate ourselves to the Mystic Law enables us, too, to attain such greatness, to rise to the summit of such glory. We are advancing bathed in the resplendent golden sunlight of the Daishonin's immense spiritual struggle.

1. In his annotations on the Nirvana Sutra.

2. *Ho'on Sho Mondan* (Commentary on "Repaying Debts of Gratitude"), p. 438.

3. At the Fourth Tokyo Youth Division Athletic Meet, held at Mitsuzawa Stadium in Yokohama, in 1957.

4. At the fifth general meeting of Soka Kyoiku Gakkai (Value-Creating Education Society; the forerunner of the Soka Gakkai) in 1942.

5. His statement appears in the *Chuhen Gikyo*, which is cited in Dengyo's *Shugo Kokkai Sho*.

6. Saicho is another name for Dengyo.

7. *Toda Josei Zenshu* (Collected Works of Toda Josei), vol. 6, pp. 459–60.

8. "Precepts for Youth" in 1951.

9. Kumarajiva accepted an invitation from Yao Hsing, king of the Later Ch'in dynasty, and came to the capital, Ch'ang-an, in 401. There he participated in the translation of numerous Buddhist scriptures from Sanskrit into Chinese.

10. A similar statement is found in the *Shotoku Taishi Den Shiki*, a work by the Tendai priest Kenshin (1130–92).

'The One Essential Phrase' (1)

People Who Chant Daimoku Are Never Deadlocked

All people share the wish to lead truly joyous lives. Everyone hopes he or she can meet death with a sense of having led a fulfilled existence. In reality, though, these aspirations are seldom met. What, then, should one do?

One of Nichiren Daishonin's disciples put the question this way: "Can one attain Buddhahood just by chanting Nam-myoho-renge-kyo?" Buddhahood is an immense state in which life is joyful and death is joyful, too. The question, in other words, is whether it is possible to attain such a wonderful state of life by simply chanting daimoku.

The lady Myoho-ama posed this candid and straightforward question, this inquiry on the most fundamental of issues, to the Daishonin. While several of the Daishonin's followers were known as Myoho-ama, the one who received this reply is thought to have lived in what is today Okanomiya in Numazu, Shizuoka Prefecture.

In the Daishonin's day, the suffix -*ama* indicated a laywoman of deep faith who, as a sign of her commitment to Buddhism, had cut her hair from waist- to shoulder-length.

Myoho-ama was in a sense asking this question as a representative of all people of the Latter Day of the Law. The Gosho we will now begin studying[1] is the Daishonin's reply. Let us study it with this in mind.

> First, for you to ask a question about the Lotus Sutra is a rare source of good fortune. In this age of the Latter Day of the Law, those who ask about the meaning of even one phrase or verse of the Lotus Sutra are much fewer than those who can hurl great Mount Sumeru to another land like a stone, or those who can kick the entire galaxy away like a ball. They are even fewer than those who can embrace and teach countless other sutras, thereby enabling the priests and laymen who listen to them to obtain the six mystic powers.[2] Equally rare is a priest who can explain the meaning of the Lotus Sutra and clearly answer questions concerning it. The *Hoto* chapter in the fourth volume of the Lotus Sutra sets forth the important principle of six difficult and nine easy acts. Your asking a question about the Lotus Sutra is among the six difficult acts. (MW-1, 221)

Nichiren Daishonin praises Myoho-ama, telling her that to ask about the Lotus Sutra is itself extremely rare and a source of great good fortune.

The Lotus Sutra explains the doctrine of the "six difficult and nine easy acts." In addition to those that the Daishonin describes here, the nine easy acts include such feats — all of them impossible from the standpoint of common sense — as walking across a burning prairie carrying a bundle of hay on one's back without getting burned. The point is that, compared with the six difficult acts, even such things are easy.

The six difficult acts are: to propagate the Lotus Sutra widely, to copy it or cause someone else to copy it, to recite it even for a short while, to teach it to even one person, to hear of the Lotus Sutra and inquire about its meaning, and to accept and maintain faith in the Lotus Sutra after Shakyamuni's passing.

Myoho-ama's asking the Daishonin about the Lotus Sutra corresponds to the noble act of inquiring about its meaning. In addition, the Daishonin points out, it is extremely rare to encounter a person who can correctly answer such a question.

Myoho-ama may well have been hesitant to pose her question, uncertain of the propriety of doing so. But the Daishonin's encouragement doubtless put her mind at ease and lifted her spirits. This was Nichiren Daishonin's way with the people.

In contrast, there are those who take others to task for asking questions, saying things like: "What's that? Don't you even know that?" There are those who put on airs of self-importance when teaching others. Such people fail to realize that they are in effect negating the Daishonin's Buddhism.

Tsunesaburo Makiguchi once remarked:

> There was a certain teacher who, when a pupil asked a question, would scold the child saying, "Don't you know that yet? You're a real numskull!" But the pupil asked the question because he wanted to learn the answer, not because he wanted to have his intelligence evaluated. This is a case of the teacher failing to recognize the demands of the situation and instead passing judgment.
>
> The blurring of the distinction between recognition of facts and judgmentalism lies at the heart of the intellectual malaise of the present age.

This is a brilliant insight.

Many of the Daishonin's letters are replies to questions from followers. The Daishonin no doubt had an air of openness and accessibility about him that made it possible for people to ask him anything.

Where there is an atmosphere of lively discussion, where people can say or ask anything, it is bright and joyful. In such an environment there is growth. The rhythm of kosen-rufu, of moving forward, is there.

While sounding extremely difficult, the nine easy acts are, for the most part, physical and external in nature, and relate to mystic powers — to what might be called "supernatural abilities." But revolutionizing one's life through following the correct teaching is in fact far more difficult than working "miracles" of this kind.

As a matter of fact, modern materialist civilization, while accomplishing countless "miracles" that were formerly impossible, has not brought about human happiness. The doctrine of the six difficult and nine easy acts sounds a stern warning against the limitations of this approach.

> This is a sure indication that if you embrace the Lotus Sutra, you will certainly attain Buddhahood in your present form. Since the Lotus Sutra defines our life as the Buddha's property of the Law, our mind as the Buddha's property of wisdom and our actions as the Buddha's property of action, all who embrace and believe in even a single phrase or verse of this sutra [i.e., Nam-myoho-renge-kyo] will be endowed with the benefit of these three properties. (MW-1, 221)

The Daishonin says that those who practice the Mystic Law will attain Buddhahood in their present form, meaning in this existence. Each of us, just as we are, will come to shine as a Buddha. This is human revolution.

The teachings expounded prior to the Lotus Sutra taught that the Buddha's body is the property of the Law; the Buddha's mind, the property of wisdom; and the Buddha's compassionate conduct, the property of action. The Buddha was always presented as an extraordinary being to be revered from afar.

By contrast, the Lotus Sutra explains that ordinary people are themselves Buddhas. This is a landmark teaching. The Lotus Sutra explains that the Buddha endowed with the three enlightened properties is the common mortal of *kuon ganjo*. Nichiren Daishonin says that when we embrace the Mystic

Law, our lives become the property of the Law; our minds, the property of wisdom; and our actions, the property of action.

Our lives are the property of the Law — this means that our lives, our determination, which is an entity of the oneness of body and mind, becomes one with the Mystic Law. Our lives or determination become the wish for realizing kosen-rufu. We can then wholeheartedly devote ourselves to others' happiness.

When we chant daimoku with appreciation at having the rare opportunity to dedicate our lives to such a noble mission, immense vitality wells forth. From the depths of our lives, we tap the wisdom to encourage others and show actual proof. And our conduct, as the Buddha's property of action, translates into value-creating activities perfectly responding to the needs of our circumstances and of those around us.

The basis for this is daimoku. Prayer — deep prayer from the very marrow of our lives. A person of deep prayer, a person who constantly chants the daimoku of Nam-myoho-renge-kyo, is never deadlocked.

The Mystic Law Is the Essential Wisdom for Becoming Happy

> Nam-myoho-renge-kyo is only one phrase, but it contains the essence of the entire sutra. You asked whether one can attain Buddhahood only by chanting Nam-myoho-renge-kyo, and this is the most important question of all. It is the heart of the entire sutra and the substance of its eight volumes.

> The spirit within one's body may appear in just his face, and the spirit within his face may appear in just his eyes. Included within the word Japan is all that is within the country's sixty-six provinces: all of the people and animals, the rice paddies and other fields, those of high and low status, the nobles and the commoners, the seven kinds of gems[3] and all other treasures. Similarly, included within the title, Nam-myoho-renge-kyo, is the entire sutra consisting of all eight volumes, twenty-eight chapters and 69,384 characters without exception. (MW-1, 221–22)

The eyes are indeed the window to the soul. The eyes express a person's life in its totality. Similarly, the immense energy of a nuclear explosion is expressed by the succinct formula $E=mc^2$.[4]

While these are merely analogies, the single phrase *Nam-myoho-renge-kyo* is the key that unlocks the limitless energy of life. The Gohonzon of Nam-myoho-renge-kyo contains all the wisdom of Buddhism and the Lotus Sutra.

Josei Toda once said: "The Gohonzon is truly great. But because this is so simple, people fail to understand it."

Because the Law is profound, its practice is simple. The more technology advances, machines become simpler to operate. Mr. Toda went so far as to liken the Gohonzon to a "happiness-manufacturing machine." And the switch for turning this machine on is chanting daimoku for oneself and others. It could be said that Nichiren Daishonin distilled Buddhism down to an essence of irreducible simplicity for all people.

It seems all too simple. When television was invented, though, people were no doubt amazed at how extremely simple and convenient it was. Now television is taken for granted; no one thinks of it as mysterious anymore. The same will be true of the Mystic Law when kosen-rufu is achieved.

President Toda predicted that 200 years later everyone would finally understand the significance of our efforts. He also said, "As science progresses, the validity and correctness of Buddhism will be increasingly borne out."

The air around us is filled with radio waves of various frequencies. While these are invisible, a television set can collect them and turn them into visual images. The practice of chanting daimoku to the Gohonzon aligns the rhythm of our own lives with the world of Buddhahood in the universe. It "tunes" our lives, so to speak, so that we can manifest the power of Buddhahood in our very beings.

The Daishonin indicates in this Gosho that Nam-myoho-renge-kyo is the heart of the entire Lotus Sutra. It is the "eye" and essential core of Buddhism. A comprehensive compilation of wisdom for helping people become happy, Buddhism has at its essence the daimoku of the Lotus Sutra, or Nam-myoho-renge-kyo.

This is why everything becomes a source of value, everything is brought to life, when we base ourselves on daimoku. The Daishonin teaches that *myo* in Nam-myoho-renge-kyo means "to revive, to return to life." Nam-myoho-renge-kyo rejuvenates all knowledge; it revitalizes our daily lives.

People today have a great deal of knowledge. But even though vast bodies of knowledge have been developed in scientific technology, psychology, sociology, economics, politics and other fields, confusion and turmoil in the world continue unabated. The words of an ancient Greek philosopher, "There are those who lack wisdom even while knowing many things," seem increasingly relevant. People today are like travelers who wander through a vast desert in search of water, unaware that there is a spring right under their feet.

We possess the essential wisdom for revolutionizing human life and manifesting great states of life. We possess the supreme jewel of humankind. Therefore, we are the people of the greatest wisdom and wealth.

President Toda said: "While people today are extremely greedy, they do not desire the vast benefit of attaining Buddhahood. On this point they could be called unselfish, people of modest wants, or just plain foolish."

With "great greed" for attaining Buddhahood, let us continue working to develop the state of life of absolute happiness — the state in which life itself is an irrepressible joy — in our own lives, while enabling friends to do the same.

1. "Myoho-ama Gozen Gohenji" (*Gosho Zenshu*, pp. 1402–03), written in July 1278, when the Daishonin was 57. Editor's Note: The Gosho text here may differ in places from what appears in the *Major Writings* or other previously published translations. This is so that the wording of the English text will accord more smoothly with the modern Japanese translation of the original Japanese Gosho. (The author is

using a modern Japanese rendering of the classical Japanese original as the basis of his lectures in this series.)

2. Six mystic powers: Expounded in the Kusha Ron, they are: 1) the power to appear anywhere at will; 2) the power to observe all phenomena in the world, no matter how large or small, near or far; 3) the power to understand all sounds and languages; 4) the power to read minds; 5) the power to know people's past lifetimes; and 6) the power to be free from all innate desires.

3. Seven kinds of gems: They differ slightly according to different scriptures. "The Emergence of the Treasure Tower," the eleventh chapter of the Lotus Sutra, defines them as: gold, silver, lapis, coral, agate, pearl and carnelian. From the standpoint of faith, they indicate the seven jewels of the Treasure Tower.

4. Energy equals mass times the speed of light squared.

'The One Essential Phrase' (2)

Prayer Is the Sun That Dispels Suffering

President Josei Toda taught that we should study Nichiren Daishonin's writings with a spirit of wholehearted conviction in their truth.

Buddhism is, in a sense, a science. Physics takes the physical world as its subject. Sociology looks at social phenomena. Psychology investigates the human psyche. By the same token, Buddhism is a science that takes life in its entirety as its subject. Happiness and suffering are what it investigates.

How can this world be rid of misery? How can each person lead the happiest life? How can that happiness and good fortune be made eternally indestructible? These are the questions that Buddhism pursues.

The vast body of all sutras, known collectively as the eighty thousand teachings, and the countless treatises and interpretations that came later, represent the progress of this investigation and its findings. The Gosho then embodies the conclusion of all this research.

Imagine someone new to the study of physics sitting in on lectures by Einstein, who stood at the pinnacle of his field. If from the outset the neophyte doubted everything Einstein said, he or she would not grow in understanding.

Therefore, President Toda taught, when we read the Gosho, we should receive it with our entire beings — with a spirit of "Yes, that's exactly right." This is the shortcut to happiness.

> Similarly, included within the title, Nam-myoho-renge-kyo, is the entire sutra [the Lotus Sutra] consisting of all eight volumes, twenty-eight chapters and 69,384 characters without exception. Concerning this, Po Chü-i[1] stated that the title is to the sutra as eyes are to the Buddha. In the eighth volume of his *Hokke Mongu Ki*,[2] Miao-lo stated that T'ien-t'ai's *Hokke Gengi* explains only the title, but that the entire sutra is thereby included. By this he meant that, although the text was omitted, the entire sutra was contained in the title alone. Everything has its essential point, and the heart of the Lotus Sutra is its title, Nam-myoho-renge-kyo. Truly, if you chant this in the morning and evening, you are correctly reading the entire Lotus Sutra. Chanting daimoku twice is the same as reading the entire sutra twice, one hundred daimoku equal one hundred readings of the sutra, and a thousand daimoku, a thousand readings of the sutra. Thus, if you ceaselessly chant daimoku, you will be continually reading the Lotus Sutra. The sixty volumes of

the T'ien-t'ai doctrine[3] present exactly the same interpretation. (MW-1, 222)

In Nichiren Daishonin's day, some carried out the practice of reading the Lotus Sutra in its entirety. The Daishonin indicates, however, that this is not necessary. He says that chanting the daimoku, or title of the sutra, once is the same as reading the entire sutra once, and that chanting a thousand daimoku is the same as reading the sutra a thousand times.

As indicated by the word *ceaselessly* in this passage from "The One Essential Phrase,"[4] the important thing is to continue the practice of chanting daimoku throughout our lives. The amount of daimoku we chant each day will naturally vary somewhat over time. That's perfectly all right. The important thing is that we continue chanting daimoku throughout our lives.

Even if someone has practiced hard for many years, if he or she should abandon faith, from that moment on his or her life will become dark — like a light that has been unplugged.

As we see here and in many other Gosho, Nichiren Daishonin invariably backs up his arguments with documentary proof. He quotes sutra passages and cites the interpretations of T'ien-t'ai, Miao-lo and Dengyo. Why?

Since the Daishonin is the original Buddha, one might suppose that he could have simply described his enlightenment directly. But had he done so, the people of his time might not have been convinced of the truth of his words. Therefore, he cites textual sources to clarify that he is not speaking arbitrarily. "My teaching exactly accords with what

Shakyamuni says, and with the interpretations of the great teachers T'ien-t'ai and Dengyo," he pointed out. "Therefore, please believe it wholeheartedly."

So when we study a passage of the Gosho where the Daishonin cites Shakyamuni's words and the interpretations of T'ien-t'ai and Dengyo, we should understand that the Daishonin, in his mercy, is trying to ensure that we, despite our strong tendency to doubt, are not confused. He is trying to give us confidence that what he says is correct.

When we can thus sense the Daishonin's immense compassion, we are deeply reading the Gosho.

> A law this easy to embrace and this easy to practice was taught for the sake of all humankind in this evil age of the Latter Day of the Law. A passage from the Lotus Sutra refers to [its practice] "in the Latter Day of the Law."[5] Another reads, "[if a bodhisattva] in the latter age hereafter, when the Law is about to perish, should accept and embrace, read and recite this sutra...."[6] A third states, "In the evil age of the Latter Day of the Law if there is someone who can uphold this sutra...."[7] A fourth reads, "In the last five hundred year period you must spread it abroad widely."[8] The intent of all these teachings is the admonition to embrace and believe in the Lotus Sutra in this Latter Day of the Law. The learned priests of Japan, China and India who have turned their backs on the true teaching have all failed to comprehend this obvious meaning. They follow

either the Hinayana or the provisional Mahayana teachings of the Nembutsu, Shingon, Zen and Ritsu sects; but have discarded the Lotus Sutra. The people do not realize that the priests misunderstand Buddhism and trust them without the slightest doubt because they appear to be true priests. Therefore, unintentionally, the people have become enemies of the Lotus Sutra and foes of Shakyamuni Buddha. From the viewpoint of the sutra, it is certain that not only will all their wishes remain unfulfilled, but their lives will be short and, after this life, they will be doomed to the hell of incessant suffering. (MW-1, 222–23)

Chanting daimoku is a teaching that is "easy to embrace and easy to practice." Anyone can perform it. It can be done anytime and anywhere. It is the most highly refined and simplified method of practice. As such, it is the perfect Buddhist teaching for not only the twenty-first century but for the twenty-second, thirtieth and fiftieth centuries, and for the ten thousand years and more of the Latter Day of the Law — for all eternity.

President Toda, smiling brightly, would say:

> If a large hospital were to concoct a treatment that, if you took it every day for an hour, would enable you to become happy without fail in both body and spirit, the place would no doubt be packed. Regardless of whether it was expensive or if you had to wait in line for hours, people would come every day to receive it.

> We can get this medicine, the mystic medicine of daimoku, in our own homes — and while sitting down, at that. All we need to pay for are candles and incense. So from the standpoint of cost, it is the least expensive method available. If someone just grumbles and fails to carry out the practice, it's a great waste.

The practice of chanting daimoku embodies the Buddha's ardent and heartfelt wish to lead all people to happiness. A practice that only certain people can carry out goes against the Buddha's spirit.

Nevertheless, the Buddhist priests of Japan, China and India have prompted people to discard the Lotus Sutra and have trampled on the Buddha's spirit. Because these aberrant priests have had the appearance of "true priests," the people have been deceived. In this Gosho, we can hear the Daishonin crying out for people to open their eyes and use their wisdom.

A follower of Buddhism ought to practice as Shakyamuni instructs. Those claiming to be the Daishonin's followers ought to do as Nichiren Daishonin says. Otherwise, they are not true followers.

False priests try to make people abide by their mistaken beliefs and opinions. This is the inherent danger in a situation where a clergy assumes the role of directing the laity.

For precisely this reason, the SGI makes the Gohonzon and the Gosho its eternal foundation. It is vital that we always practice in direct accord with Nichiren Daishonin's teaching.

Faith: the Key to Eternal Happiness

Even though one neither reads nor studies the sutra, chanting the title alone is the source of tremendous good fortune. The sutra teaches that women, evil men, and those in the realms of Animality and Hell — in fact, all the people of the Ten Worlds — can attain Buddhahood. We can comprehend this when we remember that fire can be produced by a stone taken from the bottom of a river, and a candle can light up a place that has been dark for billions of years. If even the most ordinary things of this world are such wonders, then how much more wondrous is the power of the Mystic Law. The lives of human beings are fettered by evil karma, earthly desires and the inborn sufferings of life and death. But due to the three inherent potentials of Buddha nature — innate Buddhahood, the wisdom to become aware of it, and the action to manifest it — our lives can without doubt come to reveal the Buddha's three enlightened properties. The Great Teacher Dengyo declared that the power of the Lotus Sutra enables anyone to manifest Buddhahood in their present form. He stated this because even the Dragon King's daughter was able to attain Buddhahood through the power of the Lotus Sutra. Do not doubt this in the least. Let your husband know that I will explain this in detail when I see him.

Nichiren

The third day of the seventh month in the first year of Koan (1278) (MW-1, 223–24)

Daimoku is like light. As the Daishonin says, "A candle can light up a place that has been dark for billions of years." Similarly, the moment we offer prayers based on daimoku, the darkness in our lives vanishes. This is the principle of the simultaneity of cause and effect. At that very instant, in the depths of our lives, our prayer has been answered.

The inherent cause (*nyo ze in*) of a deep prayer simultaneously produces a latent effect (*nyo ze ka*). While it takes time for this effect to become manifest, in the depths of our lives, our prayers are immediately realized. So at that moment light shines forth. The lotus flower (*renge*), in blooming and seeding at the same time, illustrates this principle of simultaneity of cause and effect.

Therefore, it is important that we offer prayers with great confidence. The powers of the Buddha and the Law are activated in direct proportion to the strength of our faith and practice. Strong faith is like a high voltage — it turns on a brilliant light in our lives.

Prayers are invisible, but if we pray steadfastly they will definitely effect clear results in our lives and surroundings in time. This is the principle of the true entity of all phenomena. Faith means having confidence in this invisible realm. Those who impatiently pursue only visible gains, who put on airs, or who are caught up in vanity and formalism will definitely become deadlocked.

In the SGI organization, the success of our activities or meetings, for example, hinges on whether the leaders have prayed thoroughly to give each person hope and for each participant, without fail, to leave the activity with a sense of profound fulfillment. Those who are only concerned with what others think of them are not qualified to be SGI leaders.

People who base themselves on prayer are sincere. Prayer cleanses and expands the heart, and instills character.

Sufferings Are the Raw Material of Happiness

Daimoku is also like fire. When you burn the firewood of earthly desires, then the fire of happiness — that is, of enlightenment — burns brightly. Sufferings thus become the raw material for constructing happiness. For someone who does not have faith in the Mystic Law, sufferings may be only sufferings. But for a person with strong faith, sufferings function to enable him or her to become happier still.

Faith is inextinguishable hope. The practice of faith is a struggle to realize our desires. And the basis of this practice is prayer. Through prayer, hope turns into confidence. This spirit of confidence unfolds in three thousand ways, finally resulting in the attainment of our hopes. Therefore, we must never give up.

Even places that have been shrouded in darkness for billions of years can be illuminated. Even a stone from the bottom of a river can be used to produce fire. Our present sufferings, no matter how dark, have certainly not continued for billions of years — nor will they linger forever. The sun will definitely rise. In fact, its ascent has already begun.

Those who over long periods grow accustomed to being miserable may acquire the tendency to give up. But with the Mystic Law we need never resign ourselves to defeat.

To put ourselves down is to denigrate the world of Buddhahood in our lives. It is tantamount to slandering the Gohonzon. The same is true of setting your mind that absolutely nothing can be done about some particular problem or suffering.

Also, we must not decide in advance that a particular person or a particular area is a lost cause. It is precisely when faced with challenging circumstances that we need to pray. The key is to offer concrete prayers and take action — until results are produced.

For instance, until a few years ago no one could even have imagined friends of the Mystic Law active in the former Soviet Union and other communist bloc countries. But the age has now changed. The long period of darkness has been broken. The starting point for this change lay in prayers for the people of those countries to definitely become happy and to shine with hope.

Prayers based on the Mystic Law are not abstract. They are a concrete reality in our lives. To offer prayers is to conduct a dialogue, an exchange, with the universe. When we pray, we embrace the universe with our lives, our determination. Prayer is a struggle to expand our lives.

So prayer is not a feeble consolation; it is a powerful, unyielding conviction. And prayer must become manifest in action. To put it another way, if our prayers are in earnest, they will definitely give rise to action.

Prayer becomes manifest in action, and action has to be backed up by prayer. Only then can we elicit a response from the Buddhist gods and all Buddhas. Those who pray and take action for kosen-rufu are the Buddha's emissaries. They cannot fail to realize lives in which all desires are fulfilled.

Even if we have so much happiness that we wish for a little suffering, our happiness continues to increase by leaps and bounds — like a kite that soars ever higher. That is the proof of attaining Buddhahood. Moreover, if we succeed in firmly establishing the world of Buddhahood in this lifetime, it will be ours eternally.

As the Daishonin indicates at the end of this letter, where he says, "Do not doubt this in the least," we need to have great confidence and live with great hope, whether we are young or old. When we manifest great hope, we can calmly survey our former sufferings. We can see that we have been taking small problems and blowing them up, worrying about them all out of proportion.

With this letter, the Daishonin appeals to all humankind: "Let us live with hope! Eternally! Our mind of faith instantaneously becomes the cause, the effect — and the power — of eternal happiness. It translates into great joy and great fulfillment."

1. Po Chü-i (772–846): Noted Chinese poet of the T'ang dynasty.

2. *Hokke Mongu Ki* (Annotations on the *Hokke Mongu* [Words and Phrases of the Lotus Sutra]).

3. Sixty volumes of the T'ien-t'ai doctrine: The three major works of T'ien-t'ai — *Hokke Gengi* (Profound Meaning of the Lotus Sutra), *Hokke Mongu* (Words and Phrases of the Lotus Sutra) and *Maka Shikan* (Great Concentration and Insight) — and Miao-lo's annotations of these. Each of these comprises ten volumes.

4. "Myoho-ama Gozen Gohenji" (*Gosho Zenshu*, pp. 1402–03), written in July 1278, when the Daishonin was 57. Editor's Note: The Gosho text here may differ in places from what appears in *The Major Writings* or other previously published translations. This is so that the wording of the English text will accord more smoothly with the modern Japanese translation of the original Japanese Gosho. (The author is using a modern Japanese rendering of the classical Japanese original as the basis of his lectures in this series.)

5. LS14, 201.

6. LS14, 203.

7. LS17, 242.

8. LS23, 288.

'Letter to Ko-ama Gozen' (1)

Respecting As Buddhas Those Who Take Action for Kosen-rufu

What is the conclusion of the Lotus Sutra? That a person who upholds the Mystic Law should be treasured wholeheartedly. The sutra says, "If you see a person who accepts and upholds this sutra, you should rise and greet him from afar, showing him the same respect you would a Buddha" (LS28, 324).

In the "Record of the Orally Transmitted Teachings," Nichiren Daishonin explains that this constitutes the "ultimate transmission" (*Gosho Zenshu*, p. 781). These words bring Shakyamuni's preaching of the twenty-eight chapters of the Lotus Sutra to a close. They represent the sutra's final conclusion.

"Letter to Ko-ama Gozen"[1] was sent to the wife of Ko Nyudo[2] of Sado Island. The *Ko* in both names is probably from the name of the place where they lived. The couple became devotees of the Daishonin while he was in exile on Sado. They were childless, and it appears they were advanced in age.

In a letter dated two months prior, Nichiren Daishonin tells the couple: "Shakyamuni Buddha, the lord of teachings, must be a compassionate father to both of you. I, Nichiren, must be your child" (MW-7, 87). And, "Because you have no sons, please consider coming here [to Minobu] to live with me in your old age" (MW-7, 88). This reveals how much the Daishonin thought of this couple who came to his aid when he was undergoing great persecution.

"When the Mongols come pouring into Japan," he tells them, "please make your way here" (MW-7, 88). He is very specific. Treasuring people means taking tangible action on their behalf.

> I have received three hundred *mon*[3] of coins from the wife of Abutsu-bo.[4] Since both of you are of the same mind, have someone read this letter to you and listen to it together.
>
> I have also received the unlined summer robe you sent to me here in the recesses of this mountain in Hakiri Village, Kai Province, all the way from the province of Sado where you live. (MW-4, 139)

The year after the Daishonin went to live at Mount Minobu, Ko Nyudo came all the way from Sado to visit him, journeying hundreds of miles over both sea and rugged terrain. According to the modern calendar, he made this journey in July. The summer heat must have made the trip extremely arduous.

Ko Nyudo brought with him offerings of 300 *mon* of coins from Sennichi-ama, the wife of Abutsu-bo, and an unlined robe from Ko-ama.

Three hundred *mon* in the Daishonin's day would have equaled the price of a large sack of rice. Sennichi-ama must have scrimped and saved to make this offering. In Ko-ama's offering of an unlined robe, we can sense her spirit of consideration for the Daishonin. She was no doubt concerned for his comfort in the hot summer weather.

After staying for a time with the Daishonin, Ko Nyudo returned to Sado and was given this letter. Since it was entrusted to Ko Nyudo, it was addressed to Ko-ama. But the Daishonin indicates that because Sennichi-ama is "of the same mind," it is the same as if he had sent the letter to her. The Daishonin tells them that they should have someone read the letter aloud to the two of them. At the time, the majority of the population was illiterate.

He uses the expression "of the same mind." We are friends and comrades practicing in the unity of "many in body, one in mind." The joy of one is the joy of all; the suffering of one is the suffering of all. And the glory of one is the glory of all.

When we base ourselves on this spirit of "one in mind," there is neither envy nor backbiting. Nor is there shirking of responsibility. Instead, we can manifest strong, broad-minded faith, and our lives will overflow with benefit.

Josei Toda said time and again, "Unity is the basis of the guidance of the Soka Gakkai."

> The *Hosshi* chapter in the fourth volume of the Lotus Sutra states: "If there is someone who seeks the Buddha Way and during a certain kalpa presses palms together in my presence and recites numberless verses of praise, because of these praises of the Buddha he will gain immeasurable blessings" (LS10, 164). This means that the benefit of making offerings to a votary of the Lotus Sutra in the evil age of the Latter Day of the Law surpasses that of serving in all sincerity as noble a Buddha as Shakyamuni with one's body, mouth and mind for an entire medium kalpa.[5] (MW-4, 139–40)

Here the Daishonin, basing what he says on the sutra, explains to these two couples, from the standpoint of Buddhism, how wondrous is their sincerity.

The votary of the Lotus Sutra in the evil age of the Latter Day is Nichiren Daishonin. This passage is saying that the benefit of praising the Daishonin is even greater than that of praising Shakyamuni for an extremely long period. This is in fact the secret of the Lotus Sutra.

For whom was the Lotus Sutra expounded? In "Essence of the Lotus Sutra," the Daishonin says, "The Latter Day is the focus of the Lotus Sutra, and Nichiren is the focus of the Latter Day" (*Gosho Zenshu*, p. 334). Fundamentally, the Lotus Sutra was expounded for the people of the Latter Day and explains Nichiren Daishonin's activities. The Lotus Sutra was expounded to predict the appearance of the original Buddha and the Gohonzon, and to prove their legitimacy.

The Lotus Sutra predicts that after the setting of the "moon" of the twenty-eight–chapter Lotus Sutra, the "sun" of Nam-myoho-renge-kyo will rise in the Latter Day.

Doubtless such an idea had never occurred to these elderly couples on Sado Island. But they were fond of the Daishonin. They had been in close contact with him and had come to respect him from the depths of their lives. An unbreakable bond had formed between them, prompting them to make many trips to visit him at distant Mount Minobu.

Leaders of kosen-rufu, too, need to be liked by their fellow members. If a leader is hated by everyone, then his or her faith is meaningless.

Almost nowhere does Nichiren Daishonin indicate that he is the original Buddha. Had he come out and directly made such a claim, probably no one would have believed him. It might even have caused people to disbelieve and slander his teaching, and abandon their faith.

The Daishonin always spread the Mystic Law based on the sutra and through his own conduct. In this letter, for example, rather than adopting a prideful, self-aggrandizing attitude, he highly praises his followers. Then, out of the desire to further encourage them, he touches on the nobility of the Lotus Sutra's votary in the Latter Day.

This is the Daishonin's spirit. How the Daishonin must lament the arrogance of priests of later generations who order people to respect them! What indignation he must feel! How he must condemn them!

Moreover, such "befuddled priests" have even persecuted the SGI, whose members have made boundless offerings to

100 • DAISAKU IKEDA

the Gohonzon. This shows how completely their actions contradict the Daishonin's Buddhism.

This is truly a "befuddled age." Recent events increasingly bear out the reality of the Latter Day. In this letter, the Daishonin gives his assurance that the benefit for those who spread the Mystic Law in such a deluded age, who stand up for kosen-rufu at such a time, is immense and boundless.

> Although this may seem unbelievable, you should not doubt it, because such are the Buddha's golden words. (MW-4, 140)

"This might be difficult to believe," he is saying, "but I am not speaking arbitrarily. It is clearly stated in the sutra. You should have the greatest confidence in this."

This is guidance that strikes a chord in the heart. The basis of guidance is to help the other person stabilize his or her mind and gain conviction and self-confidence.

> The Great Teacher Miao-lo further clarifies this passage from the sutra by saying, "If there is one who troubles [a preacher of the Dharma], then his head will be split into seven pieces; if there is one who makes offerings [to the preacher], his good fortune will surpass that of making offerings to a Buddha of the ten honorable titles."[6] In other words, the benefit of making offerings to a votary of the Lotus Sutra in the Latter Day of the Law exceeds that of making offerings to a Buddha endowed with the ten honorable titles.

> On the other hand, one who persecutes a votary of the Lotus Sutra in the impure age will have his head broken into seven pieces. (MW-4, 140)

These famous lines are inscribed on either side of the Gohonzon. Tsunesaburo Makiguchi interpreted this passage as explaining the principles of benefit and loss. Benefit produces value in life, whereas loss produces antivalue.

Benefit and loss are not imparted by someone else. When we act in accord with the Law, value is produced. When we go against the Law, we receive retribution. To use a familiar example, if someone goes outside in the severe cold of winter without wearing warm clothes, he or she might experience the loss of becoming sick.

Buddhism deepens and expands our common sense regarding the affairs of daily life and the world. It reveals the Law of life that we need to follow in order to become happy.

In his treatise "The History and Belief of the Soka Gakkai" (1951), President Toda wrote:

> Mr. Makiguchi, my mentor, would often say: "The Gohonzon has great power. This means that if you slander the Gohonzon, you will experience loss. If a father is not upstanding enough to scold his children, how can he help them to become happy? Pray to the Gohonzon sincerely. Can't you hear the Gohonzon saying to you, 'If you slander this Law, you will have your head broken into seven pieces'? This statement, which we can read on the Gohonzon, indicates the loss one will actually

experience if one commits slander." I think that Mr. Makiguchi was correct in this contention....

In the upper-left corner of the Gohonzon is an inscription that reads, "If there is one who makes offerings, his good fortune will surpass that of making offerings to a Buddha of ten honorable titles." Doesn't this signify the Gohonzon's promise to us that we will receive benefit when we revere it? Benefit, or value, and loss, or antivalue, constitute the reality of our daily lives. Some Nichiren Shoshu priests had forgotten that the power of the Gohonzon can be revealed in one's daily life — in both ways — until President Makiguchi discussed it. They were astonished at what he brought forth....

The head temple feared persecution if it supported Mr. Makiguchi's contention that unless a country, family or individual follows the teachings of Nichiren Daishonin and Nikko Shonin, it will experience loss. It seemed that the head temple was frightened of the possible persecution it would face from the military if believers did not obediently enshrine the Shinto object of worship.[7]

We should faithfully follow not the authorities but Nichiren Daishonin. This was President Makiguchi's great spirit.

Upholding the Mystic Law Brings Great Benefit

President Makiguchi cried out: "What grieves me is not just the downfall of our religion but having to stand by and watch the whole nation destroyed before my eyes.... I fear the grief it would cause Nichiren Daishonin."

Just as Mr. Makiguchi predicted, Japan was destroyed.

"His head will be split into seven pieces" indicates a state in which people lose the ability to distinguish between what is correct and what is mistaken, between what should and should not be done. It is a state where people become confused and can understand neither reason nor justice, gain nor loss.

This was the case in the Daishonin's age. And it was the state of Japan in the time of President Makiguchi. We cannot fail to recognize that, lamentably, this is increasingly the condition of Japanese society today.

An age in which people's values become distorted is a deluded age. In such a society, people encounter great persecution simply because they spread the Lotus Sutra, which teaches respect for human dignity. For precisely this reason, great benefit lies in store for those who endure this hardship and persist in spreading the Mystic Law.

The fact that the priesthood in President Makiguchi's day had forgotten the doctrine of punishment and loss indicates that it had descended into abstract theory and formalism in which Buddhism has no relevance to people's lives. The Soka Gakkai revived Buddhism as a teaching for daily life. Buddhism is not abstract — it is a teaching for triumphing over the realities of life.

Daily life is a collection of both good things (value) and bad things (antivalue). If the value or benefit in someone's life outweighs the antivalue or loss, the person becomes happy. If the opposite is true, the person is unhappy.

Faith in the Mystic Law is the wellspring of value creation. It enables us to turn everything in our lives — both our joys and sufferings — into causes for accumulating the values of beauty, benefit and good in still greater measure. When we base ourselves on this kind of faith, everything that happens to us is a benefit.

"Thank you. Truly, thank you," the Daishonin says. "I fully understand your spirit. The Buddha praises you."

One can imagine these two elderly women of Sado closing their eyes and recalling the Daishonin and the sound of his voice as they listened to this letter being read.

What a caring world! What a world rich with human warmth!

This is the true world of Buddhism. And the SGI carries on this spirit.

---

1. "Ko-ama Gozen Gosho" (*Gosho Zenshu*, pp. 1324–25), written in June 1275 when the Daishonin was 54. Editor's Note: The Gosho text here may differ in places from what appears in *The Major Writings* or other previously published translations. This is so that the wording of the English text will accord more smoothly with the modern Japanese translation of the original Japanese Gosho. (The author is using a

modern Japanese rendering of the classical Japanese original as the basis of his lectures in this series.)

2. Nyudo: A lay priest, meaning one who is tonsured but continues to live as a layman.

3. *Mon*: A monetary unit in ancient Japan. One thousandth of a *kan*, which consisted of a thousand coins strung together on a cord.

4. Wife of Abutsu-bo: Sennichi-ama. While Nichiren Daishonin was in exile on Sado, Sennichi-ama and her husband, Abutsu-bo, converted to his teaching. The couple frequently visited him in his forlorn hut at Tsukahara, bringing him food, stationery and other daily necessities. After the Daishonin was pardoned, Sennichi-ama maintained devout faith and sent her husband to visit him at Mount Minobu three times.

5. Medium Kalpa: 15,998,000 years, according to the *Kusha Ron*.

6. This is a rephrasing of the *Hokke Mongu Ki* (Annotations on the *Hokke Mongu* [Words and Phrases of the Lotus Sutra]). The ten honorable titles are: 1) "Thus Come One" (from the world of truth); 2) "Worthy of Offerings"; 3) "Right and Universal Knowledge"; 4) "Perfect Clarity and Conduct"; 5) "Well Gone" (to the world of enlightenment); 6) "Understanding of the World"; 7) "Unexcelled Worthy"; 8) "Leader of People"; 9) "Teacher of Gods and Humans"; and 10) "Buddha, the World-Honored One" (an awakened

one, endowed with perfect wisdom and virtue, who can win the respect of all people).

7. *Toda Josei Zenshu* (Collected Works of Toda Josei), vol. 3, pp. 102–03, 106. For complete English text, see *Seikyo Times*, June 1991, pp. 29–31).

'Letter to Ko-ama Gozen' (2)

A Buddhist Is a Friend to Those Suffering

Buddhism comes to the aid of those suffering. A Buddhist is the foremost ally of people who are destitute or whose lives are filled with sorrow; those who are worn out from their earnest struggles in life; who are suffering.

The SGI is strong because it is uncompromising on this point. Though we may encounter a succession of great difficulties, as long as we maintain this spirit, the SGI will always be victorious.

Nichiren Daishonin certainly didn't triumph in his struggles because he had allied himself with the powerful. Exactly the opposite was true. He loved the people, became their ally and exerted himself on their behalf. As a result, he realized victory amid great persecution.

> I, Nichiren, am the most extraordinary person in Japan. The reason I say so is this. The seven reigns

of heavenly gods I will set aside, and the five reigns of earthly gods[1] are beyond my knowledge, but throughout the ninety reigns from the time of the first human emperor Jimmu until the present, or during the more than seven hundred years since the reign of Emperor Kimmei [when Buddhism was introduced to this country], no one has ever been so universally hated as Nichiren on account of either secular or Buddhist matters. Mononobe no Moriya[2] burnt down temples and pagodas, and Kiyomori Nyudo[3] had Todai-ji and Kofuku-ji temples destroyed, but the people of their clans did not harbor hatred toward them. Masakado[4] and Sadato[5] rebelled against the imperial court, and the Great Teacher Dengyo incurred antagonism from the priests of the seven major temples of Nara,[6] but these men were not hated by priests, nuns, laymen and laywomen throughout the whole of Japan. In my case, however, parents, brothers, teachers and fellow priests — every single person from the ruler on down to the common people — treat me as if I were their parents' enemy, and show me more hostility than if I were a rebel or a robber.

Thus, at times I have been vilified by several hundred people; and at other times, besieged by several thousands, I have been attacked with swords and staves. I have been driven from my residence and banished from my province. Finally I twice incurred the regent's displeasure, being exiled once to Izu Province and again to Sado Island. When I was banished to Sado in the northern sea, I had neither provisions to sustain me nor even clothes as coarse as those made of wisteria vines to cover my body. The people there, both priests and laity, hated me even more than did the men and women of Sagami Province.[7] Abandoned in the wilderness and exposed to the snow, I sustained my life by eating grass.

I felt as though I were personally experiencing the sufferings of Su Wu,[8] who survived by eating snow while living in captivity in the land of the northern barbarians for nineteen years, or of Li Ling,[9] who was imprisoned in a rocky cave on the shore of the northern sea for six years. I underwent this ordeal not because of any fault of my own but solely because of my desire to save all the people of Japan. (MW-4, 140–42)

Josei Toda often said, "Compared to the Daishonin's suffering on Sado, our own difficulties, no matter how great they might seem, are nothing." And Tsunesaburo Makiguchi stoically endured the harrowing conditions of prison life, saying, "While it might seem that a calamity has befallen us, it is hardly a fraction of what the Daishonin underwent."

The Daishonin deliberately sought out extreme hardship for the sake of his followers in later generations. By summoning difficulties and then overcoming them, he established the eternal prime point for the widespread propagation of the Mystic Law.

It is said that good medicine tastes bitter. The "Life Span" chapter of the Lotus Sutra relates the parable of the excellent physician and his sick children. This parable describes how an excellent physician (the Buddha) tries to cure his children (all people) who have mistakenly drunk poison by giving them good medicine (the Mystic Law). But because the poison has deeply penetrated their bodies, the children, in their deluded state, do not want to take the good medicine that will effect their cure.

Although Nichiren Daishonin strove to "save all the people of Japan," not only did people, including the arrogant authorities, refuse to take the good medicine that he proffered, but they persecuted and tried to do away with him. It was truly a case of "the poison [having] penetrated deeply" (LS16, 228).

"I, Nichiren, am the most extraordinary person in Japan," the Daishonin says. He means that for having propagated the Mystic Law, he has acquired an ill repute second to none.

In this passage he describes his sadness and indignation at the deluded state of the country, and at the same time his immense compassion — not diminished in the least by the hardships he has endured — to lead all people to happiness. We also see the Daishonin's great and imperturbable confidence in kosen-rufu in the future. In addition, these words convey his pride in being the true votary of the Lotus Sutra and in having encountered the great persecutions that the sutra predicts will befall its votary in the Latter Day of the Law.

The Daishonin views himself with an objective gaze, using expressions that suggest a sense of detachment. In this we can sense the Daishonin's state of life. It is as though he is laughing heartily, from high above, at the storm of persecution unfolding beneath him. We can almost hear the Daishonin declare: "To undergo persecution for the Lotus Sutra is the greatest honor. I have won!"

> However, while I was in exile there, you and your husband Ko Nyudo, avoiding the eyes of others, brought me food by night. You were both ready to give your lives for my sake without fearing punishment from the provincial officials. (MW-4, 142)

When the Daishonin first arrived at Sanmai-do[10] in Tsukahara, Sado Island, on November 1, 1271, he was accompanied by a number of disciples. But several weeks later, he sent most of them back to the mainland. This is indicative of just how short they were on food.

Even after the Daishonin went to live in relative comfort at Ichinosawa (also on Sado), he was allowed only a meager ration, barely enough to sustain him and his disciples.

Under such circumstances, out of their sincere concern for the Daishonin, Abutsu-bo and Ko Nyudo secretly brought him food in the middle of the night. Had they been observed by the Nembutsu followers or officials who kept watch on the Daishonin's crude hut day and night, it would have been calamitous for them. Being caught supplying the Daishonin with food would have meant banishment or imprisonment.

In fact, on three occasions documents were fabricated purporting to convey government orders. These stated, for example, that any person supporting the Daishonin "should be driven out of the province or imprisoned" (MW-1, 191–92).

Some were jailed simply because they had passed in front of the Daishonin's hut; others were banished or their spouses and children arrested because they had given the Daishonin something. Abutsu-bo and his wife Sennichi-ama were fined and driven from their place of residence, which was confiscated (MW-6, 256).

Even so, Abutsu-bo and Sennichi-ama, and Ko Nyudo and Ko-ama were not afraid. The Daishonin says that at one point they were even ready to die in his place. Mentor and disciple should support each other with a willingness to face hardship.

"How can we allow our mentor to suffer alone? Let us face difficulties to lighten the burden of our mentor": That was their spirit. What wondrous people! The Daishonin says that he will never forget them in any life to come (MW-6, 258). The honor due Ko Nyudo and the Daishonin's other followers is eternal. People will sing their praises for ten thousand years, for all eternity. The Daishonin's followers will never be forgotten.

We, the members of the SGI, are creating a global foundation for kosen-rufu in the Latter Day. We are conducting activities not for the short term but with a view toward the next ten thousand years and more.

Those who struggle to the full extent of their abilities now, at this time, will also gain eternal honor. We can imagine 100 or 200 years hence, when our descendants proudly say, "Think of it, my ancestors devoted their lives to kosen-rufu in this area."

> Therefore, although life on Sado was harsh, I was loath to leave, feeling as if my heart were being left behind, and I seemed to be pulled back with each step I took. (MW-4, 142)

In another Gosho, the Daishonin says: "Though water may be muddied, it will become clear again. Though the moon may hide behind the clouds, it will surely reappear" (MW-5, 296).

On March 8, 1274, a letter of pardon from the government reached the Daishonin in his place of exile. The charges against him had been proven groundless.

It was springtime, and the seasonal flowers were racing into bloom. While the danger to the Daishonin naturally had not disappeared, for the disciples accompanying him, the journey back to Kamakura must have seemed like a proud and triumphant return.

But it pained the Daishonin to part with the people of Sado. These were friends who had joined him in life-or-death struggles, and they might never meet again. For his followers in Sado as well, with each passing day their delight at his being pardoned must have been increasingly tempered by the sadness of separation.

Of course they were overjoyed. No longer was it necessary for them to worry about officials watching them. Joining hands with the Daishonin and his disciples, they rejoiced at his vindication. At the same time, though, they shed tears of sorrow for his departure. Nichiren Daishonin and Nikko Shonin must have been deeply touched.

On March 13, the Daishonin left Ichinosawa. His followers probably wanted to accompany him as far as they could. The Daishonin may have had to tell them time and again, "Thank you for accompanying us, but you've really come far enough," urging them not to go any further.

With each few steps, the Daishonin and his disciples may have stopped and turned around to bid farewell to their Sado friends who, in turn, continued to wave until the Daishonin and his party were no longer in sight. You can easily imagine such a scene.

There is an expression in Japanese to "feel as if one's hair is being pulled from behind," which indicates a great reluctance to leave a person or place behind. The Daishonin remarks that though his head was shaven, he still felt drawn back.

He says,[11] "Although life on Sado was harsh, I was loath to leave, feeling as if my hair, though shorn, was being pulled from behind, and I seemed to be pulled back with each step I took." This brief passage is imbued with Nichiren Daishonin's irrepressible sentiments. As they listened to this letter being read, the hearts of Ko-ama and the others must have swelled with fond memories of that day.

The Daishonin sounds like someone who has left his home. Far from expressing resentment or complaints about his exile, he regrets having had to leave Sado. Nichiren Daishonin had changed his harsh place of exile into a blissful pure land of heart-to-heart friendship.

Persecutions Are an Honor

> I wonder what karmic bonds we formed in the past. Just when I was thinking how mysterious it was, you sent your most precious husband as your messenger to this distant place. I thought it must be a dream or an illusion. Even though I cannot see you, I am convinced that your heart remains here with me. (MW-4, 142–43)

The followers on Sado had carried on their faith in the midst of great persecution. Therefore, there was nothing false or fickle in their attitude. The Daishonin placed the greatest trust in them. In one passage, he goes so far as to suggest that Abutsu-bo is the reincarnation of Bodhisattva Pure Practices (Jpn. Jyogyo), one of the four leaders of the Bodhisattvas of the Earth.

Even after the Daishonin went to live at Mount Minobu, his followers in Sado made the long journey to visit him. He was visited not only by Abutsu-bo and Ko Nyudo, but also by Abutsu-bo's son, Tokuro Moritsuna, and by Nakaoki Nyudo.[12] Longing to see the Daishonin, they undertook the arduous journey to Mount Minobu — difficult to make even once — a number of times. In modern terms, this would probably be comparable to going from Japan to South America. And relatively speaking, it was even further, an even more difficult trip.

The Gosho "Letter to Zenichi-ama" describes how a follower from Sado spent an entire month serving the Daishonin at Mount Minobu, foraging, carrying water and gathering firewood for him (*Gosho Zenshu*, p. 1335).

The Daishonin and his followers shared heart-to-heart bonds. Once during a widespread epidemic, the Daishonin became deeply concerned about the Sado people. As soon as he saw the face of Abutsu-bo, who paid him a visit at that time, the Daishonin asked: "Is your wife, Sennichi-ama, OK? How is Ko Nyudo?" On learning that they were safe and well, he breathed a sigh of relief (MW-6, 257–58).

Those Who Undergo Great Persecution Together Forge Eternal Bonds

> Whenever you yearn for me, Nichiren, look toward the sun which rises in the morning and the moon which appears in the evening. I will invariably be reflected in the sun and the moon. In the next life, let us meet in the pure land of Eagle Peak. Nam-myoho-renge-kyo.
>
> Nichiren
>
> The sixteenth day of the sixth month (MW-4, 143)

Whenever one of the husbands departed from Mount Minobu, the Daishonin wrote a letter for him to take back to his wife. The Daishonin did this to praise the faith of the wife who had sent her husband on the journey. Above all, the Daishonin was keenly aware of the sadness that these elderly women must have felt knowing that they could never again meet him face to face.

"Even though you are in Sado, your heart has come here to Mount Minobu," he says warmly. "It is the same as if we had met." "Let us look forward to our meeting at Eagle Peak." "Whenever you look upon the sun or moon, your thoughts are with me."

The sun and moon can be seen from anywhere. "When you long for me," he says, "look at the sun, look at the moon. And I will be there." So great was his concern for these pure-minded followers. These words express his immense state of life. For him, it was as though the entire universe was his backyard.

The two women then, whenever they looked up at the sky — morning, midday, evening or night — probably sensed that they were gazing up at the Daishonin's merciful countenance.

Even if someone is close by, their heart may be far away. On the other hand, even if someone is far away, if there is a heart-to-heart bond, they could not be closer. The heart is what counts. In the world of the heart, there is no separation. And chanting daimoku erases distance.

President Toda, in a letter from prison to his son, who had been evacuated from Tokyo to avoid the air raids, wrote:

> I cannot see you for a while yet, but I want us to promise each other something. Sometime in the morning, whenever it is convenient for you, face the Gohonzon and chant daimoku 100 times. At the same time, I'll chant 100 daimoku, too.
>
> In this way we can communicate through the heart, just like through a wireless. We can talk with each other. We

> will create an alliance of father and son. Or we can include your mother, or grandfather and grandmother, too, if you like.

Someone who embraces faith is never isolated. The heart can communicate without fail.

The same is true of education in the home. You are busy doing activities for kosen-rufu. It may be that you cannot always be with your children. But spending a lot of time together with them is no guarantee that they will develop into fine men and women — that is another matter entirely. In fact, it sometimes happens that children whose parents spend a great deal of time with them become overly dependent and fail to develop a spirit of self-reliance.

The most noble thing is for parents to proudly teach their children a way of life of altruism and dedication to Buddhism, conveying this spirit through their lives. Forming a strong heart-to-heart bond with your children is the key to education in the home that produces outstanding individuals.

Of course, every home is different. We cannot make sweeping generalizations based on other people's situations. Spending quality time with your children is very important — but the most crucial ingredient in education is a genuine heart-to-heart bond. This is the essence.

The basis for such a bond is deep prayer. It is important to make concrete efforts to communicate your feelings and convictions to your children whenever the chance arises.

It was not authority that united the Daishonin and his followers; nor was it their concern for profit. They were united by the heart. For this reason, their bond was indestructible. For this reason, their lives overflowed with benefit and their connection was lofty and eternal.

> 1. Seven reigns of heavenly gods and five reigns of earthly gods: Native deities said to have ruled Japan before the time of the first emperor Jimmu.
>
> 2. Mononobe no Moriya (d. 587): An official who opposed the adoption of Buddhism. When an epidemic broke out, he declared that it was because of the new religion, and attempted to halt all Buddhist practice.
>
> 3. Kiyomori Nyudo (1118–81): Taira no Kiyomori, leader of the Taira clan. In 1177, he uncovered a plot against his clan in Nara and had Todai-ji and Kofuku-ji temples razed in punishment for their support of the conspirators.
>
> 4. Masakado (d. 940): Taira no Masakado, a warrior who wielded power in eastern Japan. In 939, he rebelled against the imperial court by proclaiming himself the new emperor. However, he was killed and his rebellion crushed.
>
> 5. Sadato (1019–62): Abe no Sadato, the head of a powerful family in eastern Japan. He sought independence from imperial rule but was killed in battle.

6. Seven major temples of Nara: The principal Buddhist temples in Nara, Japan's capital during the Nara period (710–94), including Todai-ji and Kofuku-ji.

7. Sagami Province: Where Kamakura, the seat of the military government, was located.

8. Su Wu (140–60 B.C.E.): A minister of the Former Han dynasty. In 100 B.C.E., Emperor Wu sent Su Wu to the land of the nomadic Hsiung-nu tribes to demand that they acknowledge fealty to him. Their chieftain rejected the demand and had Su Wu imprisoned in a cave. He endured many hardships before being able to return to the Han.

9. Li Ling (d. 74 B.C.E.): A military commander during the Former Han dynasty. During one battle, he was captured by the Hsiung-un tribes and imprisoned. When news of his defeat reached the court, Emperor Wu mistakenly believed that he had revolted against the Han, and had all the members of his family killed. Later, the emperor repented, offering to secure his return. But Li Ling refused, dying in the land of the Hsiung-nu.

10. Sanmai-do: A dilapidated shrine in the middle of a graveyard where the Daishonin passed his first winter in exile on Sado.

11. The following is a literal translation of the Gosho passage quoted earlier.

12. Nakaoki Nyudo: A follower of Nichiren Daishonin who lived at Nakaoki on Sado Island. Even after the Daishonin was pardoned and went to live at Minobu, Nakaoki Nyudo sent him letters and sought his guidance.

'Letter to the Mother of Oto Gozen' (1)

A Person of Genuine Faith Shines When Faced With Great Obstacles

It was a miraculous journey: a woman traveling all the way from Kamakura to Sado Island with her small child in tow. Going over passes, climbing mountains, crossing the sea, she appeared breathlessly before Nichiren Daishonin in his place of exile.

"It was almost too amazing to be true" (MW-3, 197), the Daishonin says. At this unexpected appearance of one of his Kamakura followers, the Daishonin probably doubted his own eyes. To a place where no visitors came, here were two — a woman with a small child!

His initial surprise soon turned to profound concern. "How was your journey?" he asked. "Did you have any trouble on the way? Is your child all right? Seeing you is the most wonderful thing. Nothing could make me happier."

The woman was a person of wholehearted faith. And doubtless she had deeply cherished the determination to see the Daishonin on Sado. "I cannot just sit idly by at this time when the Daishonin is battling great persecution," she probably felt. She must have wanted to do anything she could to lighten his burden even a little.

This letter to the mother of Oto Gozen,[1] the name of the young child, praises a mother of seeking spirit who, seven centuries ago, single-mindedly advanced one step at a time in the footsteps of her mentor.

The letter is dated only November 3, but recent research supports the view that it was written at Sado in 1273.

In May the previous year, the Daishonin wrote the "Letter to Nichimyo Shonin" (MW-3, 43–53). That letter also was to a woman who, like Oto Gozen's mother, had traveled from Kamakura to visit the Daishonin at Sado with a young child. The Daishonin praises the woman highly, even giving her the Buddhist name Nichimyo Shonin.

It is generally believed today that Nichimyo Shonin and the mother of Oto Gozen were the same person. This lecture is based on that assumption.

> To the mother of Oto Gozen:
>
> Since you revere the Lotus Sutra, you are a woman who is certain to become a Buddha. [Therefore] although in my present circumstances I am ill disposed to write,[2] I send you letters frequently. Also, I understand that you are looking after the disciples [in Kamakura]. I cannot thank you enough. (*Gosho Zenshu*, p. 1222)

"If you cannot become a Buddha," he is saying in effect, "then who can?" "If you cannot become happy, then what is the purpose of Buddhism?" This question contains the Daishonin's spirit.

In times of adversity we can understand a person's true worth. The actions of Oto Gozen's mother, Nichimyo Shonin, at the height of great persecution in which "999 out of 1,000 discarded their faith" (MW-3, 69), shine eternally. She is an eternal model for women throughout the ten thousand years and more of the Latter Day of the Law.

In the fall of 1271, when the Daishonin was nearly beheaded at Tatsunokuchi and then exiled to Sado Island, there also raged a storm of persecution against his followers. Some were incarcerated, some had their lands confiscated and some were driven out of Kamakura.

As a result of this wave of attacks, many disciples and lay followers abandoned faith. Others, who perhaps did not formally give up their faith, were inwardly defeated. And some not only abandoned faith but also maliciously reviled the Daishonin.

Certainly there were base people who betrayed their comrades and thought only of trying to protect themselves. In the end, such people wind up being trusted by no one. And, above all, they wind up unable to trust even themselves. Losing all support from both within and without, they meet pitiful ends.

But no storm, however great, could put out the fire that blazed in the life of the original Buddha. During his exile to Sado — the greatest persecution of his life — the Daishonin could say with imperturbable calm in "The Opening of the Eyes," "I, Nichiren, am the richest man in all of present-day

Japan" (MW-2, [2ND ED.] 151). He succeeded in leaving behind a monumental achievement.

"The flame in my heart for the salvation of all people burns stronger still," he announces. "The Opening of the Eyes" is the Daishonin's declaration of his spiritual victory to all his followers. This "message of light" must have illuminated their hearts when they were gritting their teeth in the face of great persecution and struggling to protect one another.

A small fire can easily be extinguished by a gust of wind. But with a large fire, it is just the opposite — the stronger the wind, the higher and more furiously it blazes. Great difficulties are a tailwind for the advance of kosen-rufu.

Shijo Kingo, to whom "The Opening of the Eyes" was entrusted, could not simply sit still in Kamakura. He struck out from the capital for Sado. And Oto Gozen's mother also undertook the journey. While an adverse wind raged throughout the land, she sought the Daishonin without a second thought for personal safety.

"How could you fail to attain Buddhahood?" (MW-3, 199), the Daishonin asks, praising her efforts to seek him out and somehow repay her debt of gratitude. "Right now, what can I do to help?" she probably wondered.

It also seems that she had been diligently looking after the Daishonin's disciples in Kamakura. And the Daishonin was profoundly grateful. "I cannot thank you enough," he says. This passage conveys his sincerity.

In recent years, though, we have seen a great many arrogant priests who take for granted others' efforts on their behalf. These priests have betrayed the Daishonin.

> Above all, your having come here, even though you are a woman, is an expression of your profound spirit of faith. Whereas in my case, I am only here because I was made to come. I feel immensely indebted. (*Gosho Zenshu*, p. 1222)

Nichimyo Shonin's actions were an expression of her earnest faith. What we set our hearts on determines everything.

She certainly did not have particularly favorable circumstances. It appears that she had been separated from her husband for some time. And her daughter Oto Gozen was still, in the Daishonin's words, an "infant" (MW-3, 53).

But taking her beloved child along, she set out on the journey. It was not uncommon at the time for women to travel alone. In contrast to the well-maintained roads like the one between Kamakura and Kyoto, however, the route to Sado was a difficult one that entailed crossing both mountains and sea. It was a journey that could take even a strong man as long as three weeks.

We can get a sense of this journey's difficulty if we consider that the trip from Kamakura to Kyoto, a much longer distance, took about two weeks. Also, the stretch of sea that must be crossed to reach Sado is typically rough. People sometimes had to wait for several weeks for the waters to become calm enough to attempt a crossing. The journey by ship was an ordeal unimaginable by today's standards.

The Daishonin is not exaggerating when he describes it as a journey "over treacherous mountains and the raging sea." "The wind and rain," he adds, "make untimely onslaughts" (MW-3, 52).

What a difficult expedition it must have been for a woman with a small child! She plodded along in the early summer heat, taking her daughter by the hand or perhaps carrying her on her back, and wearily wiping the sweat from her brow.

Our Spirit Determines Everything

Moreover, this was immediately after an incident of internal strife within the ruling Hojo clan.[3] There was much instability. The Daishonin says, "The people...are as bestial as dogs or tigers" (MW-3, 52). Also, the mountains were infested with bandits, and pirates lay in wait on the sea.

Many times, to avoid the night damp, the mother must have had to ask strangers to put them up for a night. There were probably also times when her daughter would not stop crying. Just thinking about it is heart-wrenching. "You must have felt as though you were undergoing the sufferings of the three evil paths" (MW-3, 52), the Daishonin says. That's how difficult a journey it was — but the mother was not defeated.

Why not? Because she was determined to walk the same path to Sado that the Daishonin had walked. She wanted to shoulder the same hardships as her mentor. How admirable! How beautiful and noble!

Faith makes people strong. And people of genuine faith shine the most when they encounter great difficulties. Certainly, it is better not to have obstacles. But from another standpoint, difficulties are benefits. By challenging and overcoming them, we can forge a character of pure and immutable "gold."

Even if all the leaves on a tree should fall off in a strong wind, as long as the branches and trunk remain intact, in time the tree will again produce flowers. Likewise, the spread of Buddhism will continue as long as there remain people of genuine faith. The important thing, therefore, is to raise one person of genuine faith.

The Daishonin praised the mother of Oto Gozen, saying, "You are undoubtedly the foremost votary of the Lotus Sutra among the women of Japan" (MW-3, 52). And he gave her the name Nichimyo Shonin.

Nichi is from Nichiren, meaning sun, and *myo* is the first part of *myoho*, or Mystic Law. He adds the honorific title Shonin, meaning sage or saint. We see that distinctions between priestly and lay, male and female, did not matter in the least to Nichiren Daishonin; he fixed his gaze solely on people's hearts, their spirit.

Spirit means inner state of life, or one's heart. It decides what we devote our lives to. It is the fundamental prayer on which we base our existence. A person's spirit is invisible but becomes manifest at a crucial moment. Not only that, it also controls everything about a person, each moment of every day — it is the fundamental determinant of one's life.

The Kegon Sutra says, "The heart is like a skilled painter." Like a great painter, the heart freely creates representations of all things. One's heart is the designer, the painter, the sculptor and the architect of his or her being.

The Great Teacher T'ien-t'ai cites this sutra passage in explaining the doctrine of a life-moment possessing three thousand realms. He uses the image of a great painter to explain that the heart manifests in the three thousand realms of all phenomena.

It is our spirit, our life-moment, that counts. Our spirit is our hopes, our prayers. And it can also be identified with the subconscious.

"What kind of future do I envision?" we may ask ourselves. "What kind of self am I trying to develop? What do I want to accomplish in my life?" We should paint this vision of our lives in our hearts as specifically as possible. This "painting" becomes the design for our future. The power of the heart enables us to actually execute a wonderful masterpiece in accordance with that design. This is the doctrine of a life-moment possessing three thousand realms.

The more specific and detailed the blueprint we have in our hearts, the better. The point is to continue vividly painting the target we have and to advance toward that goal single-mindedly. Then, at each instant, the reality of our lives will gradually approach the painting that is our aspiration.

Everything depends on what is in our hearts. Heartfelt prayers will definitely be answered. If we decide that something is impossible, then, consistent with our minds in thinking so, even things possible will become impossible. On the other hand, if we have the confidence that we can definitely do something, we are already one step closer to achieving it.

In accordance with the principle of a life-moment possessing three thousand realms, pessimistic thoughts or feelings take form, just as they are, in reality, producing negative results. People who have negative thoughts create effects for themselves that perfectly match their thinking.

So it is important to be optimistic. There is no such thing as pessimism in Buddhism. The Lotus Sutra gives us the key that enables us to possess great confidence and burn with hope even amid circumstances that appear despairing. Nichiren Daishonin proved this with his life.

Amid the desolate conditions of Sado, the Daishonin says that he feels "great joy." These words in fact conclude "The Opening of the Eyes."

In a letter to his follower Sairen-bo, which he also wrote on Sado, the Daishonin calmly promises, "Although the lord of Kamakura may continue to refuse to pardon Nichiren, I will call upon the heavenly deities, and when I have returned to Kamakura, I will write to you" (MW-7, 27). True to his words, the Daishonin returned triumphantly to Kamakura. His victory over incredible odds is proof of the principle of a life-moment possessing three thousand realms.

Above all, I am confident that the Daishonin's resolve for world kosen-rufu in the ten thousand years and more of the Latter Day was the cause that resulted in the appearance of the SGI, and it called forth Bodhisattvas of the Earth throughout the world.

The power of our hearts is great. Nichimyo Shonin's heart was directed toward the Daishonin. And from him, she learned to share the Lotus Sutra's ideal of all people becoming happy.

She was determined to travel to far-off Sado, even though it meant crossing mountains and treacherous waters. I hope that each of you will steadfastly advance one step at a time toward a great ideal, walking along roads, traveling over mountains and crossing seas, as need be, to reach it.

The Daishonin says, "Even common mortals can attain Buddhahood if they cherish one thing: earnest faith" (MW-1, 268).

We need to direct our spirit, our hearts, toward kosen-rufu. Attaining Buddhahood depends on cherishing such resolve. When we have such a spirit, our lives sparkle with jewels of good fortune and happiness. We undertake a wonderful journey through life in which our dreams, one after another, are accomplished.

>1. "Oto Gozen no Haha Gosho" (*Gosho Zenshu*, pp. 1222–23): thought to have been written in November 1273, when the Daishonin was 52.

>2. The original Japanese could also be interpreted as meaning, "Although I am not much of a letter writer…."

>3. In 1272, Hojo Tokisuke, an elder half brother of the ruling regent, Hojo Tokimune, plotted to seize power. But Tokimune discovered the plot and swiftly suppressed it by having his brother killed.

'Letter to the Mother of Oto Gozen' (2)

We Gain Fortune With Every Step We Take for the Mystic Law

Having faith produces benefit and good fortune not limited to this lifetime but spanning past, present and future. The eternity of life, the eternal law of cause and effect, is a solemn reality. Believing in the "Life Span" chapter of the Lotus Sutra means living with confidence in this reality.

> Among the many disciples of Shakyamuni Buddha, there were ten known as the ten major disciples.
>
> Among these, Maudgalyayana[1] was the foremost in supernatural powers. He could travel anywhere in the four continents[2] and in the entire realm beneath the sun and moon, in less time than it takes to cut a single hair.

> When we inquire into the cause for his gaining such powers, we find that in a past life he would travel as far as a thousand miles in order to hear Buddhism being expounded.
>
> Also, Chang-an, the disciple of the Great Teacher T'ien-t'ai, managed to make his way 10,000 miles[3] to become the apprentice of T'ien-t'ai and to hear about the Lotus Sutra. The Great Teacher Dengyo journeyed 2,000 miles[4] in order to study the *Maka Shikan*.[5] The Tripitaka Master Hsüan-tsang[6] traveled 200,000 miles [from China to India] and acquired the Prajna (Hannya) sutras.
>
> [When we consider these examples,] it seems that the length of the journey traveled in pursuit of the Law represents the strength of seeking spirit. (*Gosho Zenshu*, pp. 1222–23)[7]

People who use their legs, who move around for the sake of Buddhism, gain the good fortune and benefit with which to freely travel the world. People who prepare places for Buddhist meetings, including those who clean the community and training centers, develop the state of life to dwell in "bejeweled houses" in the future. These examples are not fairy tales. The Mystic Law is wondrous and inscrutable. This is a function of the law of the simultaneity of cause and effect.

Actions taken for kosen-rufu cannot fail to produce effects. If we are confident of this — and to the extent that we have this confidence — effects will manifest without fail. But if our confidence is partially clouded by doubt, then we will only see vague or indistinct results, like the light of a half moon.

The path that the mother and her daughter, Oto Gozen, traveled was not simply a road. It was the path for attaining Buddhahood, the path for accumulating boundless good fortune and benefit.

"The length of the journey traveled in pursuit of the Law represents the strength of seeking spirit," the Daishonin says. Even though it might be difficult, when you thoroughly advance in pursuit of Buddhism, with every step you plant more seeds of good fortune and benefit in your life. These will, as a matter of course, eventually flower and bear fruit.

All of you have worked hard for many years to achieve kosen-rufu. And you continue to take action. How the Daishonin must praise your spirit!

To illustrate how our daily efforts accrue, take the case of someone who delivers the *Seikyo Shimbun* every day to a mailbox on the fourth floor of a building. In just climbing those flights of stairs every day for two years, this person will have ascended to a cumulative height greater than Mount Everest.

Or if a district women's division leader walks for activities a mile every day for ten years, she will have walked approximately 3,650 miles. In fifteen years she will have covered more than 5,475 miles.

As for the journey from Kamakura to Sado, while there will be some variance depending on how you calculate it and how you determine the specific route taken, the distance, including ascents and descents over mountainous terrain, probably came to between 250 and 312.5 miles. All the women's division members are "present-day mothers of Oto Gozen." They are people with a mystic mission.

Our spirit changes our being. It changes our lives. Why does the Buddha have an indestructible, diamond-like life? Shakyamuni explains it is because he has steadfastly and thoroughly protected the True Law. Having a strong spirit for kosen-rufu enables us to develop diamond-like lives. The boy who offered a mud pie to Shakyamuni was later reborn as King Ashoka.

There are now many members who have developed the state of life with which to freely travel the world, thanks to having painstakingly walked countless narrow lanes and alleys to encourage friends during the early days of our movement. It may be that those responsible for the sound system at meetings, as a result of the good fortune and benefit they gain thereby, are creating the cause to be reborn as great musicians.

In activities for kosen-rufu, absolutely no effort is wasted. Everything is engraved in our lives and enables us to establish a diamond-like and totally free state of life. In overcoming our weaknesses and exerting ourselves daily for our friends, we have already achieved victory as human beings. Ultimately, our victory or defeat in life is not decided by someone else — we decide it. A person who steadfastly adheres to the path he or she has chosen is a winner.

> These people were all men. They were regarded as reincarnations of Buddhas or bodhisattvas. But you are a woman. And, moreover, you probably are unfamiliar

> with the comparison between provisional and true Mahayana and other such doctrinal matters.
>
> Your having come all the way here to Sado despite this must be due to the roots of goodness you created in past lives. (*Gosho Zenshu*, p. 1223)

The individuals the Daishonin mentions, whose names shine in Buddhist history, were courageous people who sought the Law even at the cost of their lives. He says that the mother of Oto Gozen has joined the ranks of these great predecessors. What a landmark teaching this is!

His words fly completely in the face of the accepted beliefs of his day. They erase the formidable distinctions between men and women, and among reincarnations of Buddhas and bodhisattvas and ordinary believers who aren't well schooled in Buddhist doctrine. The Daishonin says that the mother of Oto Gozen is a woman who is certain to become a Buddha. Differences in gender and social status have nothing to do with it. Nor is fame a factor. Faith, a seeking mind, is what counts.

Buddhism is a teaching beyond the secular realm. *Realm* in this case means difference or distinction. Beyond the secular realm means Buddhism transcending such superficial distinctions. It means seeing the truth of life directly, setting aside all differences. It is to observe one's mind, to see the human being.

Human society, as viewed with this eye of Buddhism, takes on a completely different meaning from that discerned by secular eyes. No longer are the powerful above and ordinary people below. Status does not make people great, and authority does not make them noble. Instead, it is people wholeheartedly dedicated to a lofty ideal who shine the brightest.

Again, as the Daishonin indicates, through "roots of goodness" the bond uniting those who advance together along the path of kosen-rufu is not solely of this lifetime.

> It is said that in the past there was a woman who so longed for the man she loved that she walked a thousand miles. There are also examples of others who, driven by such passion, transformed themselves into stones, trees, birds or snakes.[8]
>
> Nichiren
>
> The third day of the eleventh month (*Gosho Zenshu*, p. 1223)

The Daishonin mentions here a woman who longed so much for a man that she walked a thousand miles — and there are other accounts of women turning themselves into stones, trees, birds or snakes owing to such intense yearning. These didn't actually happen, but it seems to me the point is that the person's inner state of life became a rock, a tree or a snake. In this sense, you can think of countless examples of the same thing happening today. These images might seem overly dramatic, but they convey the extreme pain that people go through.

Here the Daishonin is making a comparison — while women of legend turned into stones or snakes because of their longing for someone of the opposite sex, the mother of Oto Gozen will become a Buddha because of her longing for the Lotus Sutra.

In "Letter From Sado," the Daishonin writes: "[Human beings] give their lives for shallow, worldly matters but rarely for the noble cause of Buddhism. Small wonder they do not attain Buddhahood" (MW-1, 34). Not only have we been lucky enough to be born as human beings, but we have had the rare fortune to encounter the correct Buddhist teaching. By firmly establishing in our hearts a strong yearning for kosen-rufu, we can manifest a state of happiness in the eternal dimensions of past, present and future. We can each become a Buddha.

And if we succeed in becoming Buddhas, then we can lead our loved ones to enlightenment, too. Together we can enjoy lives of boundless happiness.

A Mother Sows the Seeds of Happiness for Her Children

> [Postscript:] How Oto Gozen must have grown! Your efforts in service to the Lotus Sutra will no doubt fill Oto Gozen's entire life with happiness.[9]
> (*Gosho Zenshu*, p. 1223)

The Daishonin was always concerned about Oto Gozen's development. In a letter several years later ("The Supremacy of the Law"), he says, "I would imagine your daughter, Oto, has become a fine and intelligent young girl" (MW-3, 202). This child had been brought up by a true "mother of kosen-rufu."

Surely the growth of such a child is a source of great anticipation and joy.

Elsewhere, the Daishonin expresses delight at the fine growth of Nanjo Hyoe Shichiro's son Nanjo Tokimitsu, Abutsu-bo's son Tokuro Moritsuna, Toki Jonin's son Iyo-bo and others.

The Daishonin means here that the mother's good fortune and benefit in having devoted herself to the Lotus Sutra has become her daughter Oto Gozen's good fortune. The good fortune and benefit we create by exerting ourselves in faith will definitely manifest in the lives of our children, grandchildren and all our family members.

Buddhism is the supreme medicine. The Daishonin says that the benefit of faith extends to the "preceding seven generations and the seven generations that followed" (MW-7, 172).

How the Daishonin's words must have put Oto Gozen's mother at ease! For a mother, the future of her child is a matter of the greatest concern. That was probably all the truer for Oto Gozen's mother, because she was raising her daughter alone. The original Buddha promises this mother that her daughter, whose life she certainly held as dear as her own, would become happy. Thus embraced in the Daishonin's mercy, she must have felt as though all her troubles and sufferings had vanished instantly.

Oto Gozen's mother steadfastly maintained her faith. When the Daishonin moved to Mount Minobu, she undertook another journey to visit him. And later, according to one source,[10] with Oto Gozen she visited the Daishonin's successor, Nikko Shonin, after his painful departure from

Mount Minobu. Mother and daughter possessed a pure and honest seeking spirit.

When people were filled with apprehension at the impending second Mongol invasion of Japan, the Daishonin called out to the mother and daughter: "Should any calamity befall us, you should immediately come to visit me here [Mount Minobu], where you will be welcomed wholeheartedly. Should the worst happen, then let us starve together among these mountains" (MW-3, 202). "Let us suffer this calamity together," he is saying in effect. "Let us eternally share the joys and sufferings of life together."

The Daishonin never forgot the immense sincerity and concern Oto Gozen's mother showed when he was undergoing the greatest of hardships on Sado. He indicates here that he would put his life on the line to protect her and her daughter. Bonds of the heart forged in times of great difficulty are eternal. Could there be any greater honor? Could there be any greater treasure? This mother and daughter undertook a journey over mountains and across the sea, and in the end possessed a brilliantly shining jewel in their lives.

As we cross mountains and rivers together in the journey of kosen-rufu, every step of the way a symphony of eternal jewels, eternal dramas and brilliant paintings resounds in our hearts.

1. Maudgalyayana: Also known as Mahamaudgalyayana.

2. Four continents: Those situated respectively to the east, west, north and south of Mount Sumeru, according to the ancient Indian worldview. They represent the entire world.

3. The distances in this paragraph are intended figuratively, not literally.

4. Some sources indicate that he traveled three thousand miles. In China, Dengyo became a disciple of Tao-sui of the T'ien-t'ai school.

5. *Maka Shikan* (Great Concentration and Insight): One of T'ien-t'ai's three major works, compiled by his disciple Chang-an. It elucidates, among other things, the principle of a life-moment possessing three thousand realms.

6. Hsüan-tsang (602–64): A Chinese priest of the T'ang dynasty and a translator of Buddhist scriptures. He journeyed to India in 629 to study Buddhism.

7. "Oto Gozen no Haha Gosho" (*Gosho Zenshu*, pp. 1222–23), thought to have been written in November 1273, when the Daishonin was 52.

8. There are many Japanese fables and legends that portray women whose love or yearning for a man was so powerful that they turned themselves into some nonhuman or inanimate

form. This is done either to be close to that person or to wreak revenge on him for being spurned.

9. This translation is based on new research on the original writings of Nichiren Daishonin. It differs substantially from the version in the *Gosho Zenshu*.

10. *Gosho Zenshu* appendix, "Deshidannato Retsuden" (List of Disciples and Followers), compiled by the fifty-ninth high priest, Nichiko, p. 8.

'Letter to Lord Toki'

Noblest Are Those
Who Love Humanity

Shakyamuni Buddha was a traveler. Throughout his life, he was continually active and on the move.

"I will visit that place — for there are people there." Spurring himself to action, he walked on, his gaze fixed on the distant horizon. Shakyamuni sincerely loved human beings.

As he made his way through each place, he must have thoroughly enjoyed encountering new friends and discovering new qualities and virtues in old friends. Transcending all superficial differences, he drew out each person's goodwill and created heart-to-heart bonds of benevolence. Weaving such a spiritual fabric was undoubtedly his greatest joy. His spirit was that of a true champion of humanism.

A Buddhist text relates how Shakyamuni once came upon an abandoned sick man. Shakyamuni would not forsake him. He approached the man, who was filthy, and warmly comforted him. Helping him up, Shakyamuni led him outdoors and washed him. While the man was bathing, Shakyamuni even changed his bedding. Those observing this wondered why the Buddha was going to such lengths for the sick man. "If you wish to serve the Buddha," Shakyamuni told them, "then you should tend to the sick."[1] This is a well-known anecdote.

Sickness is not merely a physical phenomenon; it invariably signals the presence of spiritual malady, too. In seeking to cure someone's illness, we should spare no effort, leave no stone unturned. In the above instance, Shakyamuni's intention was probably to indicate that the path of Buddhism lies solely in working and taking action among people.

Because Shakyamuni loved people, many gathered around him, drawn by his thoroughly humane conduct. And, naturally, the atmosphere around him was always lively and bright. The same was true of the Daishonin. In his presence, people doubtless felt free to voice their innermost thoughts and feelings.

Nichiren Daishonin was of course a strict mentor and teacher. But at the same time, from his many letters, we can see that people felt absolute assurance in confiding in him. He knew everything about them.

In the Daishonin's presence, even adults would become as honest and open as children. Almost without realizing it, they would reveal their genuine, unaffected selves, their true faces.

Toki Jonin was one such follower. From the Daishonin's letters to him, we can infer that Toki Jonin must have been very concerned about his mother. And the Daishonin respected and treasured his feelings. He gave him the support and encouragement he needed to conduct himself with true filial devotion toward his mother.

In the Gosho we are studying this time,[2] we can sense the Daishonin's immense spirit of love and humanity.

> I have received one unlined kimono.
>
> Among the Buddha's disciples there was one monk who, when the Buddha was in a place where there was famine and was restricted in his activities because of the shortages, sold his clerical robes and gave the money that he received to the Buddha.
>
> The Buddha asked him where the money had come from. So the monk told him how he had acquired it, relating everything exactly as it had happened.
>
> The Buddha then declined the offering, saying: "The surplice is the Dharma robe for the enlightenment of all Buddhas over the three existences. I do not have the power to requite such an offering." So the monk asked, "Then what should I do with the money that I received for my surplice?" In response, the Buddha asked him, "Do you have a dear mother?" When the monk replied that he did, the Buddha told him, "You ought to offer this money from the surplice to your mother."
>
> The monk then said to Shakyamuni: "The Buddha is the most venerable being in the threefold world. He is the eye of all living beings. Even if it were a robe

> broad enough to wrap in itself the entire universe, or a surplice large enough to cover the earth, the Buddha is certainly worthy of such an offering. My mother is as ignorant as a cow and more thoughtless than a sheep. How could she possibly be worthy of the offering of a surplice?"
>
> The Buddha replied: "Who gave birth to you? Your mother did. Doesn't she therefore fully deserve to receive the offering of this surplice?" (*Gosho Zenshu*, p. 968)

This episode vividly conveys the humanism of Buddhism. It portrays the spirit of a disciple to want to assist his mentor, and the concern of the mentor for the disciple as well as the disciple's mother. It is a beautiful story.

It may be that, by rights, a monk was not supposed to sell his clerical robes under any circumstance. Still, the disciple took this action to support his mentor, even if it meant being reprimanded. While fully appreciating the spirit of his disciple, the Buddha tells him in effect: "I am not worthy to receive this precious offering. And, there is someone more suitable than I: That is your mother.

"Is there anyone more noble than your mother? You are carrying out Buddhist practice and will eventually become a Buddha. Therefore, to treasure the mother who gave birth to you is itself Buddhism." Buddhism teaches such true filial virtue.

Elsewhere, the Daishonin tells another major disciple, Nanjo Tokimitsu:

> One's debt to his or her father is so great as to make Mount Sumeru appear small. One's debt to his or her mother is so profound as to make even the ocean seem shallow. You should set your mind on repaying your debt of gratitude to your father and mother. (*Gosho Zenshu*, p. 1527)

I am reminded here of President Toda's "Precepts for Youth." Mr. Toda cried out to youth: "Stand tall! Join the battle with me!":

> We must fight with love for the people. Today, there are many youth who don't even love their parents, so how can they love others? Our struggle is for human revolution — to surmount our lack of compassion and develop in ourselves the mercy of the Buddha.[3]

President Toda was very strict with young people who were disrespectful toward their parents.

Shakyamuni cherished the image he had of his mother (who is said to have died when he was seven days old) and treasured his adoptive mother. The Daishonin also treasured his mother, and successfully prayed for her life to be extended when she was ill.

In the above passage, the mentor teaches a disciple who thinks his mother is ignorant and worthless that this is far from the case.

The noblest person in the world is the one with the greatest love for the people. A truly wise person is not someone who orders others to treat him or her deferentially, but someone who teaches through words and actions that each person, as well as that person's mother, is vitally important. The disciple here, suddenly grasping the immense warmth of his mentor's spirit, must have felt he was gazing upon the sun's brilliance.

The heart of one person moves another's. A Greek philosopher teaches that hatred of language and ideas leads to hatred of humanity.[4] If your heart is closed, then the doors to other people's hearts will also shut tight. On the other hand, someone who makes all those around him or her into allies, bathing them in the sunlight of spring, as it were, will be treasured by all.

A Buddhist's way of life has to embody such clear and natural reasoning. The Buddha transmits the heart's sunlight universally to all beings.

Even when we strive to treat everyone with love and compassion, though — since we are ordinary people — it is only natural that we will have likes and dislikes. There is no need for us to struggle to make ourselves fond of people we find disagreeable. In our work as emissaries of the Buddha, however, we must not let our thoughts or actions be colored by any discrimination or favoritism.

Through offering sincere prayer and conducting earnest dialogue, all of you are working to open the lives of people whose hearts are closed tight like clams. Your actions are noble.

Why do you suppose the Daishonin brings up this episode to Toki Jonin, devoting two-thirds of this short letter to it? The reason becomes clear as we keep reading.

No Effort Is Wasted

This unlined kimono was a present given by a merciful mother, more than 90 years old, to you, her beloved son [Toki Jonin]. She must have strained her eyes and expended her life to make it.

As the son, you must have sent it to me knowing that it would be difficult for you to repay the debt for this robe. And it will also be difficult for me, Nichiren, to repay it. Even so, I do not think it would be proper for me to return it.

That's because if I wear this robe and report these matters in detail before the god of the sun, then they will without fail be known to Taishaku, Bonten and all the Buddhist gods. It is but one robe, but all heavenly deities throughout the universe will surely acknowledge your meritorious conduct. Like dew joining the ocean, or soil being added to the earth, your good fortune will not be lost in lifetime after lifetime, nor decay in world after world.

With my deep respect,

Nichiren

The fifth day of the second month
(*Gosho Zenshu*, p. 968)

When the Daishonin saw the robe that Lord Toki had sent, he must have fondly recalled the face of his follower's mother. The Daishonin is said to have spent time at Toki Jonin's manor after the Matsubagayatsu Persecution in 1260. Probably he had grown close to Lord Toki's mother.

More than ten years had passed since then. In those days, a person over 90 would have been extremely long-lived. The Daishonin must have been concerned about how difficult needlework would have been for Toki Jonin's mother. His sentiments are expressed in the sentence, "She must have strained her eyes and expended her life to make it."

Toki Jonin was 60 at the time. But even after reaching an advanced age, the parent, as they say, is still the parent and the child is still the child. Toki Jonin no doubt wondered how he could reply to his mother's warm consideration.

"That's it," he probably thought, "I'll offer the robe to the Daishonin. Both he and my mother will be pleased." While there is no way of knowing whether this was his intent, the unlined kimono was delivered to the Daishonin.

The Daishonin's sense of gratitude may well have been accompanied by some hesitance. He couldn't nonchalantly accept an item that was invested with such profound love. The tale that the Daishonin relates in this reply sheds light on his feelings.

Although he was reluctant to accept the garment, to return it would amount to rejecting the sincere spirit with which it had been offered. Under the circumstances, the Daishonin acknowledges Toki Jonin's sincerity and conveys the greatest thanks and encouragement to the latter's mother.

The Daishonin says that by his wearing this robe, Bonten, Taishaku and all heavenly deities would know the ardent spirit of mother and son in making the offering. He says that the Buddhist gods in the ten directions would definitely protect them. And he concludes the letter telling them that their benefit in making such an offering would illuminate their lives in lifetime after lifetime, eternally.

What joy the mother and son must have felt on receiving this response! Toki Jonin, in his joy at conducting himself in the most dutiful manner toward his mother, must have felt the deepest gratitude to the Daishonin.

"What matters is one's heart" (MW-5, 289). Here we see a beautiful exchange take place: a mother who undertakes painstaking effort out of concern for her son; a disciple who is motivated by concern for his mother and his mentor; and the mentor who, out of his concern for the mother and son, does his utmost to bring out the best in all their efforts. This is the world of Buddhism.

The year after this letter was sent, in February 1276, Toki Jonin's mother died with him, his wife and other relatives watching over her. According to one account, she was 93 when she died.

Toki Jonin held an important position in society [as a vassal of Lord Chiba, governor of Shimosa province (present-day Chiba Prefecture), with a rank comparable to that of a steward], and was also a central figure among the Daishonin's followers.

Toki Jonin's wife also looked after his mother attentively.

One of his mother's grandchildren struggled for kosen-rufu at the Daishonin's side, and later two of her grandchildren were active under Nikko Shonin. Embraced by the mercy of the original Buddha, the life of Toki Jonin's mother was surely one of great satisfaction and victory. It was the drama of a woman who, though ordinary and without any special distinction, lived earnestly and realized victory. Buddhism exists to help such valiant individuals become happy.

When we base our lives on the great wish for kosen-rufu, regarding each effort as "like dew entering the ocean, or soil being added to the earth," then our petty lesser selves give way to the greater self that shines with eternal victory. Our every effort turns into an ocean of benefit, an earth of good fortune.

I hope each of you will be confident that, just as Nichiren Daishonin promises, you have already entered this path. And that, therefore, you will treasure your heart of faith.

The "Letter to Lord Toki," while short, is pervaded with warmth. In it, we glimpse a warm heart-to-heart exchange between the Daishonin and his followers. Because of their bond with the Daishonin and the sense of inner security that this brought, his followers could endure ordeals and struggle for kosen-rufu with all their might.

"How can I help others experience joy? How can I help them practice in high spirits and really exert themselves?" It goes without saying that someone who gives no thought to these questions and does not respond to members' needs is not qualified to be a leader in the humane world of Buddhism.

Our practice has to be based on strong prayer for the happiness of each person. Donning Toki Jonin's robe, which was imbued with sincerity, the Daishonin, too, prayed to the Buddhist gods.

When we sincerely pray, without fail the Buddha wisdom to know how to encourage others will well forth. Our movement of kosen-rufu is to expand this world of encouragement.

1. *Vinaya-pitaka*: One section of the *tripitaka*, a collection of treatises on discipline.

2. "Toki Dono Gohenji" (*Gosho Zenshu*, p. 968), written in February 1275 when the Daishonin was 54.

3. *Toda Josei Zenshu* (Collected Works of Josei Toda), vol. 1, pp. 59–60.

4. Plato, "Phaedo" in *The Portable Plato*, trans. Benjamin Jowett, ed. Scott Buchanan (New York: Viking Press, 1973), p. 238.

'A Letter of Condolence'

The Buddha Shares Others' Sufferings

A strong person is gentle. "Birds cry, but never shed tears. I, Nichiren, do not cry, but my tears flow ceaselessly" (MW-1, 94). Nichiren Daishonin wrote these famous words while in exile on Sado Island. He had great and abounding compassion. He was the perfect embodiment of profound feeling and towering wisdom.

Dostoevsky writes, "Great ideas spring not so much from noble intelligence as from noble feeling."[1]

Buddhism is a religion of compassion and wisdom — these are inseparable. A person of true wisdom has unparalleled compassion. A person of deep compassion embodies the wisdom of Buddhism.

The Japanese word for compassion, *jihi*, includes the meaning of suffering together or crying out in sympathy with others. The Buddha first of all shares others' sufferings.

Take the case of a mother whose child has died, who is sitting in a daze on the roadside. Probably no words can heal her heart. And passersby, unable to do anything, will have no choice but to walk briskly past. Occasionally, a cleric may stop before her and try to instruct her with a look of affected enlightenment. But no one can truly share her grief.

No matter how science advances, even though it can send a human being into outer space, it cannot assuage a mother's sorrow. Maybe only the words of a woman who has been in the same situation can reach her.

What would the Buddha do in such an instance? He would probably sit down at the mother's side. And he might simply continue sitting there, not saying a word. Even if no words were exchanged, the mother would sense the warm reverberations of the Buddha's concern. She would feel the pulse of the Buddha's life. Eventually, she would lift up her face, and before her eyes would be the face of the Buddha who understands all her sorrows. The Buddha would nod and the mother would nod in reply.

Even without words, there is no greater encouragement than heart-to-heart exchange. On the other hand, even if a million words are spoken, nothing will be communicated in the absence of heartfelt exchange.

At length the Buddha would stand up, and the mother, as though following his example, would probably also rise. Then, together, they would move forward one step, then another — their way gently illuminated by the light of the moon. The Buddha would tirelessly offer encouragement, until the mother could lift her head high, until she could determine to lead a life of great value for the sake of her deceased child.

The Buddha is sometimes gentle, sometimes stern, sometimes offering bouquets of words and sometimes taking action with those suffering. To the mother, the Buddha is a true ally, for he empathizes with her sufferings and brings her the greatest peace of mind. For this reason, the Buddha's words penetrate her life.

At its roots, compassion is the spirit to suffer alongside and pray with those suffering. The Daishonin possessed such a spirit. He joined Ueno-ama Gozen, the mother of Nanjo Tokimitsu (Lord Ueno),[2] in her grief and tears when her youngest son, Shichiro Goro, died at the tender age of 16. He continued to offer her encouragement until she regained the will to go on living.

During the first year or so after Shichiro Goro's death, the Daishonin sent approximately ten letters to the Nanjo family. We can imagine how his deep concern must have warmed their grieving hearts.

Starting with this installment, we will begin studying a number of letters sent to the Nanjo family by the Daishonin — and the human drama that they tell.

Letter to a Bereaved Family

> On the matter of the death of Nanjo Shichiro Goro, all people, once born, are certain to die. This is known to all people, both the wise and the foolish, both those of high and low standing. Therefore, when that time comes, one should not lament or be alarmed as though learning this for the first time. I have borne

this in mind myself and also taught it to others. But since the time has actually arrived, I cannot help wondering even now whether this [Shichiro Goro's death] is a dream or fantasy. (*Gosho Zenshu*, p. 1567)[3]

Just as there is the drama of joy upon the birth of a child, there is the drama of grief upon the death of a loved one. In the fall of 1280, these two dramas played out one after the other in the Nanjo family.

The drama of joy was the birth of a son. In a letter dated August 26 of that year, the Daishonin expresses his delight to Nanjo Tokimitsu and his wife on their being blessed with a son in addition to their infant daughter. The Daishonin named the boy Hiwaka Gozen (*Gosho Zenshu*, p. 1566).

It must have been deeply moving for the couple that the name he selected contained the Chinese character for the word *sun* (Jpn. *hi*), which forms part of the Daishonin's name, Nichiren (i.e., the same character is also pronounced *nichi*). This was one year after the Atsuhara Persecution,[4] and they must have felt that the weariness from their difficult struggles had in an instant been swept away. Above all, Tokimitsu's mother, Ueno-ama Gozen, was deeply moved by the birth of a grandson who would succeed as head of the family, and by the Daishonin's congratulatory message.

But only ten days later, on September 5, the Nanjo household was visited by misfortune. Tokimitsu's youngest brother, Shichiro Goro, died suddenly. He was only 16. While the cause of his death is unknown, it must have been very sudden and unexpected. Their celebration of the birth of a son and grandson was overturned, replaced by sorrow at Shichiro Goro's death. The family's grief knew no bounds.

The Daishonin, too, was surprised by this turn of events. As soon as the messenger bearing news of Shichiro Goro's death arrived, the Daishonin immediately wrote a reply to Tokimitsu, the "Letter of Condolence," which we are studying this time, dated September 6.

The impermanence of life is inescapable. In Buddhism, this is a fundamental premise about the nature of existence. Why should death come as a shock? From the standpoint of life's eternity, it could be said that birth and death are occurrences of minuscule significance. That is all well and good in theory, but the human heart cannot fully come to terms with such events through theory alone.

The Daishonin was thoroughly human, a most humane person. Hearing the unexpected report, he was in disbelief. He wondered whether it was "a dream or fantasy." Further on, he indicates that he is in such turmoil he doesn't feel up to continuing to write. These words must have expressed the feelings of the bereaved family members as well.

In the letter "Sad News of Lord Goro's Death,"[5] which is thought to have been written to Nanjo Tokimitsu about a week later, the Daishonin says:

> Until now I have repeatedly thought to myself that the matter of Nanjo Shichiro Goro's death must have been a dream or a fantasy, or certainly untrue, but it is again mentioned in your letter. And so, for the first time, I have become convinced of its truth. (*Gosho Zenshu*, p. 1566)

The Daishonin says that he has had a hard time accepting Shichiro Goro's death. What compassion the original Buddha shows! He mourns the death of this young follower, just as a parent would.

The Daishonin inscribed his immense compassion for all humankind in the Gohonzon. He says: "Suffer what there is to suffer, enjoy what there is to enjoy. Regard both suffering and joy as facts of life and continue chanting Nam-myoho-renge-kyo, no matter what happens" (MW-1, 161). Just as he says, in both times of joy and times of sadness, everything will turn out for the best if we continue chanting daimoku.

Someone may expound a fine teaching while abiding in a place of comfort and safety — but that is not Buddhism. A genuine Buddha lives among the people, grieves and suffers with them and shares their hopes and laughter. That's how the original Buddha, Nichiren Daishonin, conducted himself.

Above all, the Daishonin did not blithely brandish theories of karma. Making condescending pronouncements to suffering people like, "That's just your karma," will only add to their misery. Someone battling destiny feels like there is a gale raging through his or her heart. When we encounter people in such a state, we should stand with them in the rain, become sopping wet with them, and work with them to find a way out of the storm. In the end, that's probably all another human being can do.

Even if the attempt is not totally successful, through making this effort we forge a bond between ourselves and the other person. This is not mere sympathy or sentimentality. The effort to regard someone else's suffering as our own and thus offer prayer for its resolution creates a life-to-life bond. Through this bond one person touches another's life.

'Eternal Family' of the Mystic Law

Above all, how your mother [Ueno-ama Gozen] must be grieving. She was preceded in death both by her parents and siblings, and she was bereaved of her beloved husband. Still, her many children must have been a comfort to her.

[Shichiro Goro] was a charming child and, moreover, a boy. He was very handsome and brave and had a trustworthy look. He made others feel refreshed. His having died so young, however, while defying reason, is like the buds of a flower being withered by the wind, or the full moon suddenly waning.

It doesn't seem real to me [that he has died], and so I do not feel inclined to continue. I will write you again.

With my deep respect,

Nichiren

The sixth day of the ninth month of 1280

Postscript: When I met him on June 15, he struck me as a lad of splendid spirit and as very gallant. I am most sad that I will not be able to see him again.

Still, since he believed deeply in Shakyamuni Buddha and the Lotus Sutra, in his last moment he was splendidly composed. He certainly went to the pure land of Eagle Peak where his father dwells. They must have had a joyful reunion. How wonderful! How wonderful! (*Gosho Zenshu*, pp. 1567–68)

Ueno-ama Gozen had experienced a great deal of suffering. Her husband, Nanjo Hyoe Shichiro, died in 1265. He was still in the prime of his life and ought to have had many years ahead of him. He was survived by five sons and four daughters, all still young when he died; Tokimitsu, the second son, was only 7. Shichiro Goro, the youngest child and fifth son, was still in his mother's womb when his father died. In another Gosho, Nichiren Daishonin writes to Ueno-ama Gozen:

When your husband, the late Lord Ueno, preceded you in death, he was still in the prime of life and your grief on that occasion was no shallow matter. Had you not been pregnant with his child, I know you would have followed him through fire and water. Yet when this son was safely born, you felt that it would be unthinkable to entrust his upbringing to another so that you could put an end to your life. Thus you encouraged yourself and

> spent the following fourteen or fifteen years raising your children. (MW-7, 247–48)

The child to whom he refers is Shichiro Goro, who had now suddenly died. The mother looked forward to the growth of Tokimitsu and Shichiro Goro with high hopes. Shichiro Goro was handsome, intelligent and well-liked by others. It also appears that he was very dutiful toward his mother.

It seems as though even the Daishonin was at a loss as to how to encourage the mother. He conveys his feelings openly and candidly. The mother, her heart made sensitive by sadness, must have keenly felt the Daishonin's kindness, which pervades each line of the condolence letter he sent to the Nanjo family via Nanjo Tokimitsu. How the Daishonin's warmth must have consoled her grief-stricken heart! Simply having someone who understands everything can give us the strength to go on living.

In the postscript, the Daishonin reiterates his regret at the death of this youth who had such a promising future.

When Nanjo Hyoe Shichiro died, the Daishonin wrote: "While he was in this world, he was a living Buddha, and now, he is a Buddha in death. His Buddhahood transcends both life and death" (MW-2 [2ND ED.], 207).

The Daishonin teaches that someone who embraces the Mystic Law, even though his or her life may be short, is a Buddha in both life and death. In the postscript to "A Letter of Condolence," the Daishonin says that without doubt Shichiro Goro has been reunited with his father at Eagle Peak.

In another letter, he writes to Ueno-ama Gozen:

LEARNING FROM THE GOSHO • 163

> You must feel that if only [your son Shichiro Goro] had left word where you could go to meet him, then without wings, you would soar to the heavens, or without a boat, you would cross over to China. If you heard that he was in the bowels of the earth, then how could you fail to dig through the earth?
>
> And yet there is a way to meet him readily. With Shakyamuni Buddha as your guide, you can go to meet him in the pure land of Eagle Peak. (MW-7, 262)

The Daishonin tells Ueno-ama Gozen that she can definitely meet her son at Eagle Peak. Time and again, the Daishonin offers her warm encouragement.

It is extremely difficult to understand the impact that losing a child has on a mother. Even now, I cannot forget how my mother looked when she received official notification that my eldest brother had died in the war. She turned away, her shoulders went limp and her body seemed fraught with grief. My mother did not cry in front of us, but I had the clear sense that from that day she aged considerably.

Such is the cruelty of war. I will fight with my life to oppose war, which plunges mothers the world over into sorrow and grief.

For the happiness of all mothers and children, for the creation of a society where they can all look up at blue skies with smiling faces — toward this end, we are striving to develop a great undercurrent of compassion in society. This is the great objective of our movement.

1. Fyodor Dostoevsky, *The Eternal Husband*, trans. Constance Garnett (London: William Heineman, 1917), p. 105.

2. Ueno is the name of a village near Mount Fuji of which Nanjo Hyoe Shichiro, and later his son Nanjo Tokimitsu, was steward. Lord Ueno refers to the head of the family; at the time of this writing, Nanjo Tokimitsu.

3. "Ueno Dono Gohenji" (*Gosho Zenshu*, pp. 1567–68), written in September 1280 when the Daishonin was 59. It is addressed to Nanjo Tokimitsu (Lord Ueno).

4. Atsuhara Persecution: A series of threats and acts of violence against followers of Nichiren Daishonin in Atsuhara Village near Ueno, beginning in 1278. The persecution culminated in 1279 when three farmers were executed for refusing to abandon their faith. Nanjo Tokimitsu used his influence to protect believers during this time, sheltering some in his home and negotiating for the release of others who had been imprisoned. The government punished him for his role by levying severe taxes on his estate, forcing him to live in poverty.

5. "Nanjo Dono Gohenji" (*Gosho Zenshu*, p. 1566).

Two Letters to Ueno-ama Gozen

1. 'Clear Sake Gosho'

If I Don't Protect Them, Who Will?

In Buddhism there is no sentimentality. Buddhism is neither idealism nor formalism. It is a dedicated struggle to help people who are suffering become happy, to fill their hearts with new strength and life force so they can declare, "No matter what, I will survive!"

So Buddhism is an all-out, earnest struggle. There is no place in Buddhist practice for an easygoing or lackadaisical attitude. Having a position in the organization or social standing does not mean we can automatically give others hope. Only by waging a great inner struggle, with the spirit to expend our very lives, can we truly encourage others.

When Nanjo Tokimitsu's younger brother, Shichiro Goro, suddenly died, Nichiren Daishonin was nearing the end of his own life. Despite his physical infirmity, the Daishonin continued sending Tokimitsu and his mother, Ueno-ama Gozen, letters of encouragement.

What lengths the Daishonin went to for his followers! In his actions we see his spirit to resolutely protect all who embrace the Mystic Law, his determination for the well-being of all his followers, and his firm conviction: "If I don't protect them, who will?" Through his example, it seems to me, the Daishonin teaches the proper attitude for all Buddhist leaders.

The Great Light of Daimoku Illuminates Past, Present and Future

A certain sutra passage says that children are one's enemies.[1] Perhaps there is reason for this. The bird known as the owl devours its mother, and the beast called *hakei*[2] destroys its father. A man called An Lu-shan[3] was killed by his son, Shih Shih-ming [actually, An Ch'ing-hsu], and the warrior Yoshitomo killed his father, Tameyoshi.[4] Thus the sutra has grounds for saying that children are one's enemies.

Another sutra passage says that children are a treasure. King Myoshogon[5] was destined, after his life had ended, to fall into the hell called the great citadel of incessant suffering, but he was saved by his son, the crown prince Jozo. Not only was he able to escape the sufferings of that great hell, but he became a Buddha called Sal Tree King. A woman called Shodai-nyo, for the faults of greed and stinginess, was confined in the realm of hungry spirits, but she was saved by her son Maudgalyayana

and was freed from that realm.[6] **Thus the sutra's statement that children are a treasure is in no way false. (MW-7, 261–62)**[7]

Four months had passed since the death of Shichiro Goro, Ueno-ama Gozen's youngest child. Although the new year had arrived, the mother's sorrow had not yet healed. On January 13, 1281, the Daishonin sent her this letter, the "Clear Sake Gosho."

The new year can be thought of as the start of spring. At the outset of the letter, the Daishonin, as though echoing the mother's sentiments, writes: "The blossoms that once fell are about to bloom again, and the withered grasses have begun to sprout anew. Why does the late Goro not return as well?" (MW-7, 261).

He then explains that, for a parent, in some cases a child becomes an enemy and in other cases a treasure. He backs up this assertion with examples from the Buddhist sutras and history. Like the sons of King Myoshogon and Shodai-nyo, respectively, there are children who save their parents. Lord Goro had undoubtedly been such a son, the Daishonin declares.

The Lotus Sutra expounds the oneness and simultaneous enlightenment of parent and child. Children, through faith, can definitely cause their parents to attain Buddhahood. In this scenario, from the parent's perspective, the child is not merely a child but what Buddhism calls a "good friend," someone who leads another to Buddhism. In the same way, the child can also attain Buddhahood through the parent's faith. It all depends on the parent's resolute faith and nothing else. It is important that we have unshakable confidence in this.

We should chant with the determination to lead our children, as well as our parents, to happiness and complete fulfillment. Each daimoku we chant with such determination becomes a brilliant sun illuminating the lives of our children or parents, transcending great distances and even the threshold of life and death.

People wanting to have a child may tend to imagine that if only they could they would be happy. But — as the Daishonin indicates when he says that a child may become a parent's enemy — countless people become miserable on account of their children. Happiness or unhappiness in life does not hinge on whether we have children.

For that matter, those who do not have children can love and look after that many more children of the Buddha with the same parental affection they would show their own children. This is most worthy of respect.

Also, some agonize because they cannot have children. And they may be deeply hurt by someone even casually needling them about "starting a family." When it comes to such highly personal matters, we should exercise great sensitivity and discretion.

Time and Again We Will Be Reunited

> The sutra states, "If there are those who hear the Law, then not a one will fail to attain Buddhahood."[8] This means that even if one were to point at the earth and miss it, even if the sun and moon

should fall to the ground, even if an age should come when the tides cease to ebb and flow, or even if flowers should not turn to fruit in summer, it could never happen that a woman who chants Nam-myoho-renge-kyo would fail to be reunited with her beloved child. Continue your devotion to faith and bring this about quickly! (MW-7, 262–63)

"You will definitely meet your son at Eagle Peak," the Daishonin tells Ueno-ama Gozen. He first seeks to give her confidence, saying that her son has certainly attained Buddhahood. Next, he gives her hope, encouraging her that she can certainly meet her son again.

From the standpoint of life's eternity over past, present and future, when people are separated by death it is as though one of them has merely gone a short distance away. This could even be likened to someone going to another country, making it impossible to see the person for a while.

Once at a question-and-answer session, a member whose child had died asked President Toda whether it was possible, in his present life, to re-establish a parent–child relationship with his dead child. Mr. Toda replied:

> It's impossible to say for certain whether you will meet your child again during your lifetime. When I was 23, I lost my daughter, Yasuyo. All night, I held my dead child in my arms. I had not yet taken faith in the Gohonzon. I was beside myself with grief and slept with her in my embrace.

So we were separated, and I am now 58. When she died she was 3, so if she were alive now, I imagine she would be a full-grown woman.

Have I or have I not met my deceased daughter again? This is a matter of perception through faith. I believe that I have met her. Whether one is reunited with a deceased relative in this life or the next is a matter of faith.

That day my daughter died was the saddest in my life. Throughout the night, I lay sobbing, holding her cold body close to me.

Let me add something else. Never has the world been filled with such sorrow for me as it was then. One day at my office in Meguro, I thought to myself, "What if my wife were to die?" And that brought me to tears. And then my wife, too, died. Later I wondered what I would do if my mother died. I was, of course, very fond of my mother. Pursuing things still further, I shuddered at the thought of my own death.

While in prison during the war, I devoted some time to reading the Lotus Sutra. One day I suddenly understood; I had finally found the answer. It took more than twenty years to solve the question of death. I had wept all night over my daughter's death and dreaded my wife's death and the thought that I, too, would die. Because I finally could answer this riddle, I became president of the Soka Gakkai.[9]

On another occasion, Mr. Toda said: "It is not a given that you will be reunited as parent and child. It sometimes happens that the person is reborn as someone close by, though not in your immediate family."

We are connected by the invisible life-to-life bonds of the Mystic Law. We are the family of the original Buddha. We are eternal comrades.

Transcending life and death, time and again we will be reunited in the garden of our mission and renew our connection with each other. Life is hopeful and death is hopeful, too. Ours is a brilliant journey across eternity!

In any event, death is a certainty. No one can escape it. Therefore, it's not whether our lives are long or short, but whether, while alive, we form a connection with the Mystic Law — the eternal elixir for all life's ills — that, in retrospect, determines whether we have led the best possible lives. By virtue of our having formed such a connection, we will again quickly return to the stage of kosen-rufu.

The important thing is that surviving family and friends live with dignity and realize great happiness based on this conviction. Their happiness shows that they have conquered the hindrance of death and eloquently attests to the deceased's attainment of Buddhahood.

2. 'ON MY SICKNESS'

From the seventeenth day of the sixth month of the eleventh year of Bun'ei (1274), when I retired here [Mount Minobu], through the eighth day of the twelfth month of this year [1281], I have not ventured away from this mountain. For the past eight years I have become weaker year by year because of emaciating sickness and old age, and my mental powers have waned.

I have been ill since the spring of this year, and with the passing of autumn and arrival of winter I have grown weaker by the day, and each night my symptoms have grown more severe. For more than ten days now I have hardly been able to eat anything. Meanwhile the snow grows deeper and I am assailed by the cold.

My body is as cold as a stone, and the coldness in my breast is like ice. At such times, I warm up some sake and consume *kakko*,[10] and it's as though a fire has been kindled in my heart, or like entering a hot bath. Sweat washes my body and the droplets cleanse my feet.

As I was happily thinking about how I might respond to your sincerity, tears welled up in my eyes....

> While I, Nichiren, have been refraining from responding to letters from people on account of my illness, I am so saddened by this matter [of Shichiro Goro's death] that I have taken up my brush to write you. I, too, shall not be long in this world. I believe that I will certainly meet Lord Goro. If I should see him before you do, then I will inform him of your grief. (*Gosho Zenshu*, pp. 1583–84)[11]

The Spirit to Struggle for Others at All Times

The Daishonin describes his condition without embellishment. He is entirely unaffected; he makes no attempt to make himself appear to others as somehow special. In so doing, he reveals true greatness.

What sense does it make for ordinary people of the Latter Day of the Law to put on airs? What can they possibly stand to gain? We should focus instead on the self, polishing the self and striving always to live with honesty and sincerity, modesty and humility.

Since we are human, we will as a matter of course undergo the four sufferings — birth, aging, sickness and death. The important thing is that we withstand the onslaught of these sufferings and overcome them with true nobility.

Several years before this letter was written, the Daishonin wrote with calm detachment to Abutsu-bo of Sado Island: "I was born and since I have already reached nearly 60, there is no doubt that I have also experienced aging. Sickness and death are all that remain" (*Gosho Zenshu*, p. 1317). What a lofty state of life! It is as though he is calmly looking down on the dark clouds of sickness and death from blue skies high above.

The Daishonin wrote this letter to Ueno-ama Gozen in December 1281 — just ten months before his death — in response to an offering of food and medicine she had sent knowing that he was physically weakened and not eating. The offering included unpolished rice, clear sake and medicinal herbs for use as stomach medicine.

He describes his physical condition in detail. This suggests just how grateful the Daishonin must have been for Ueno-ama Gozen's sincerity. He may have taken her gesture of concern as an indication that she had recovered from her grief at her son's death and regained the capacity to respond to others' needs.

More than a year had passed since Shichiro Goro had died. Time, it is said, is an excellent physician that eventually cures all ills. Even so, a void in the heart cannot easily be filled.

The Daishonin again touches on Shichiro Goro's passing, sharing Ueno-ama Gozen's sorrow. He concludes the letter by telling her in effect, "If I should die before you do, then I will meet the late Lord Goro and tell him of your sorrow."

When he wrote this letter, the Daishonin had grown so weak and emaciated that he didn't even feel like taking up his writing brush. He does so in this case not simply to express his gratitude for the offerings but as an indication of how highly he treasures Ueno-ama Gozen's feelings. No doubt he wanted to write her even if it meant pushing himself unreasonably.

The Buddha continually prays for people's happiness. The verse section of the "Life Span" chapter of the Lotus Sutra reads:

At all times I think to myself:
How can I cause living beings
to gain entry into the unsurpassed way
and quickly acquire the body of a Buddha?
(LS16, 232)

This prayer of the Buddha concludes "Life Span." The Buddha, twenty-four hours a day, day after day and month after month, is constantly concerned about others' well-being. Continually and unswervingly, he sends people encouragement. This is the world of Buddhahood.

We who have embraced the Gohonzon should struggle to thoroughly protect all the people in our communities and organizations — to help them become happy, stand up and receive benefit. We should do so with the spirit of this passage, "At all times I think to myself...." Everything depends on leaders having such a sense of responsibility.

Leaders must always have the sensitivity and compassion to lend a hand where help is needed. They must also give guidance that is both warm-hearted and reasonable. The Daishonin's encouragement is a model for all Buddhists and for all leaders in society.

Embraced by his mother's strong faith, Nanjo Tokimitsu overcame a severe illness and went on to live to 74. In Buddhism, everything has meaning. It may be that Shichiro Goro "bequeathed" his own life span to Tokimitsu.

Carrying on the flame of his father and younger brother, Tokimitsu dedicated his life to kosen-rufu in keeping with the vow he made during his youth. And his magnificent life also attests to the victory of his mother and Shichiro Goro.

1. A paraphrase of the Shinjikan Sutra, vol. 3. The passage mentioned in the next paragraph, which says that children are a treasure, is taken from the same text.

2. *Hakei*: A legendary beast resembling a tiger that is said to eat its father.

3. An Lu-shan (705–757): a military officer in China during the T'ang dynasty.

4. Tameyoshi and Yoshitomo: Warrior leaders of the Minamoto clan who in 1156 fought on opposing sides in a conflict involving the imperial family.

5. Myoshogon: Wonderful Adornment, a king who appears in "Former Affairs of King Wonderful Adornment," the twenty-seventh chapter of the Lotus Sutra.

6. This story is described in the Urabon Sutra (see MW-7, 167). Maudgalyayana is also known as Mahamaudgalyayana.

7. "Ueno-ama Gozen Gohenji" (*Gosho Zenshu*, pp. 1575–76), written in January 1281 when the Daishonin was 60. He wrote this letter in response to an offering of various items from Ueno-ama Gozen, the mother of Nanjo Tokimitsu and Shichiro Goro. At the beginning of the letter he lists her various offerings; the first item mentioned is clear sake (Japanese rice wine), hence the title.

8. Lotus Sutra, the "Expedient Means" chapter.

9. Josei Toda, *Toda Josei Zenshu* (Collected Writings of Josei Toda) (Tokyo: Seikyo Shimbunsha, 1982), vol. 2, pp. 174–75.

10. *Kakko*: A medical herb, *tamalapatra* (sandalwood) fragrance.

11. "Ueno Dono Haha Gozen Gohenji" (*Gosho Zenshu*, pp. 1583–84), written in December 1281 when the Daishonin was 60.

'The Ultimate Teaching Affirmed by All Buddhas of Past, Present and Future'

Life Transcends Both Birth and Death

What, ultimately, is Buddhism? The Buddhist canon encompasses an immense number of scriptures, known as the eighty-four thousand teachings. And then there are also countless commentaries. Trying unaided to come to terms with such a monumental body of material is like journeying through a vast jungle without a map.

However, Nichiren Daishonin clearly states, "The eighty-four thousand teachings are the diary of one's own life" (*Gosho Zenshu*, p. 563). The Buddhist sutras, in other words, are a record, a diary, of one's life. "They are about you," he is saying. "There is nothing at all in the sutras that does not pertain to your life."

> To conceive of life and death as separate realities is to be caught in the illusion of birth and death. It is deluded and inverted thinking.

> When we examine the nature of life with perfect enlightenment [the true enlightenment of one awakened from the dream of illusions], we find that there is no beginning marking birth and, therefore, no end signifying death. Doesn't life as thus conceived already transcend birth and death?
>
> Life cannot be consumed by the fire at the end of the kalpa, nor can it be washed away by floods. It can be neither cut by swords nor pierced by arrows.
>
> Although it can fit inside a mustard seed, the seed does not expand, nor does life contract. And although it fills the vastness of space, space is not too wide, nor is life too small. (*Gosho Zenshu*, p. 563)[1]

Death is an issue of the greatest importance for all people without exception. No one can honestly say that death is of no concern. At the same time, however, few important issues are given so little serious consideration. It is said that there are two things people cannot gaze at directly: the sun and death.

The French philosopher Blaise Pascal (1623–62) decried people's tendency to avoid thinking of their own mortality: "This negligence in a matter where they themselves, their eternity, their all are at stake, fills me more with irritation than pity; it astounds and appalls me."[2] His dismay at people's irrational indifference toward death drove him to use such strong words.

What is death? What becomes of us after we die? Failing to pursue these questions is like spending our student years without ever considering what to do after graduating. Without coming to terms with death, we cannot establish a strong direction in life. Pursuing this issue brings real stability and depth to our lives.

Many views of life and death have been articulated over the ages by religious leaders, philosophers and scientists. Without going into a detailed discussion, I think it's fair to say that human knowledge has not advanced sufficiently to either definitively affirm or deny the possibility of life after death. Science takes as its object of investigation phenomena discerned with the five senses; what happens after death is beyond its purview. Its basic stance disqualifies it from speaking on the matter one way or the other.

No view of the nature of existence can offer direct proof of what happens after death. It seems, therefore, that rather than trying to compare the relative merits of different views, it is far more fruitful to ask how a particular view influences people's lives in the present — whether it makes them strong or weak, happy or miserable.

Buddhism teaches that life is eternal. It encourages us to use this existence to thoroughly polish the eternal entity of our lives. Eternal happiness, it explains, lies precisely in making such efforts.

With the view that life continues eternally over past, present and future, accomplishing human revolution becomes the ultimate purpose. When we polish and revolutionize our lives, then life is joyful — and death is joyful, too. We will also experience happiness in our future lives. What else can we call eternal?

In a letter to his follower Shijo Kingo, Nichiren Daishonin says, "No matter how dearly you may cherish your estate, when you die, it will only fall into the hands of others" (MW-3, 238). You should not jealously cling to your possessions, the Daishonin says. All too often, people fail to fully come to terms with their mortality and as a result become attached to things that ultimately have no worth.

In his *Essays*, the French Renaissance philosopher Montaigne (1533–92) introduces the following episode about a king of ancient Greece who was planning to conquer Italy:

> When King Pyrrhus [of Epirus, 319–272 B.C.E.] was undertaking his expedition into Italy, Cyneas, his wise counselor, wanting to make him feel the vanity of his ambition, asked him: "Well, Sire, to what purpose are you setting up this great enterprise?" "To make myself master of Italy," he immediately replied. "And then," continued Cyneas, "when that is done?" "I shall pass over into Gaul and Spain," said the other. "And after that?" "I shall go and subdue Africa; and finally, when I have brought the world under my subjugation, I shall rest and live content and at my ease."... Cyneas then retorted, "tell me what keeps you from being in that condition right now, if that is what you want. Why don't you settle down at this very moment in the state you say you aspire to, and spare yourself all the intervening toil and risks?"[3]

The source of this anecdote is Plutarch's *Lives of the Noble Grecians and Romans*. Pascal and others in later ages have cited it.

The point is that people find contemplating their lives and facing mortality so distasteful that they instead look for one thing after another in which to absorb themselves. Thus avoiding the essential point of polishing their lives, they arrive finally at death without having prepared in the least for that moment. The King Pyrrhus anecdote teaches the folly of such a life.

Tolstoy wrote:

> Death is more certain than the morrow, than night following day, than winter following summer. Why is it then that we prepare for the night and for the winter time, but do not prepare for death. We must prepare for death. But there is only one way to prepare for death — and that is to live well.[4]

"To live well" means to develop, cultivate and elevate our lives. Socrates called this "attending to one's soul." His famous words to the effect that "philosophy is practice for dying" carry the same meaning.

In the Gosho we are studying this time, Nichiren Daishonin teaches that the eternal entity of our lives cannot be burned by fire, corroded by water or destroyed by weapons. The eternal entity can both fuse with the universe in all its vastness and take the minuscule form of a mustard seed. It truly exists in the perfectly free state of nonsubstantiality (Jpn. *ku*).

Buddhism teaches how we can gain firm control over the function and power of the free, unimpeded aspect of life — the power of the Mystic Law. This is the teaching that a single life-moment possesses three thousand realms. Herein lies the ultimate meaning of faith.

We possess within us indestructible life force equal in power to the universe. When we tap this life force, there are no sufferings or worries that we cannot overcome.

What Is True Transcendental Power?

> People, confused by their minds, fail to understand and awaken to the true nature of their lives. The Buddha is awakened to and manifests the wondrous workings of life, which he has called "transcendental." By transcendental he means "in command of all laws of life, unobstructed by anything." This free transcendental power exists in the lives of all sentient beings. Therefore, foxes, raccoon dogs and the like can manifest their respective transcendental powers. This is the [expression of] their relative enlightenment.
>
> It is from this single entity of life that the differences among lands arise. (*Gosho Zenshu*, p. 563)

True transcendental power is not along the lines of so-called supernatural abilities. It is actually the ability to help others become happy. Nichiren Daishonin says, "Aside from the attainment of Buddhahood, there is no 'secret' and no 'transcendental power'" (*Gosho Zenshu*, p. 753).

Manifesting true transcendental power means thoroughly polishing the eternal essence of our lives, elevating ourselves toward the state of Buddhahood. By so doing, we can realize eternal happiness and develop our state of life to where we can help others become happy, too.

It may be that supernatural abilities enable people to fly. But the ability to fly won't make us happy. For that matter, to fly all we need to do is get on an airplane.

As the Daishonin indicates where he says, "It is from this single entity of life that the differences among lands arise," society and even the land change depending on the state of life of people living there. The power to change even the environment exists in the heart.

A great human revolution in the life of one person can change the destiny of humankind and the planet. It is Buddhism, the Lotus Sutra, that encourages and enables people to become aware of this great power, to draw it forth and use it. Buddhism gives people the means to develop themselves thoroughly and opens their eyes to the limitless power inherent in their lives.

Through training hard, an athlete can bring out hidden strengths and abilities to the maximum. Similarly, the extent to which we can manifest our latent power, the true essence of our lives, depends on our practice. The requisite discipline is Buddhist practice — it is faith. With the view of life existing eternally over past, present and future, establishing solid faith becomes the fundamental concern. We should make establishing solid faith our main purpose in this existence.

The Daishonin says: "Explaining the wonder of life is the prime objective of all the sutras. One who is awakened to the workings of the mind is called a Thus Come One" (*Gosho*

Zenshu, p. 564). Buddhism reveals the "wonder of life" from a wide variety of angles. Attaining Buddhahood is the same as gaining a full understanding of this wonder.

The Buddha Fully Grasps the Wonder of Life

> Explaining the wonder of life is the prime objective of all the sutras [that Shakyamuni preached], termed the eighty-four thousand teachings. These doctrines all exist in one's life. Accordingly, the eighty-four thousand teachings are the diary of one's life.
>
> We hold and embrace the eighty-four thousand teachings in our lives. To suppose that the Buddha, the Law and the pure land of Eagle Peak exist apart from one's life and to seek them outside is a delusion. (*Gosho Zenshu*, pp. 563–64)

The Buddhist sutras, again, are said to number eighty-four thousand. This is because human beings supposedly have eighty-four thousand earthly desires; the sutras are to explain the means for overcoming these.

The sutras are a record of the Buddha's life. But the Daishonin also says, "The example of one person represents the impartial truth inherent in all human beings" (*Gosho Zenshu*, p. 564). The sutras are a diary of each person's life. Whether we can believe this, whether we can remember this, depends entirely on us.

Buddhism was expounded for each of us. By fully comprehending the wonder of life, we gain complete, total freedom. We have no sufferings we cannot overcome, no prayers that are not answered. We gain all the good fortune and enter the journey of eternal life in which living is a joy and dying is joyful, too.

Happiness does not exist outside us. It is found within, in our own state of life.

Yet modern civilization continually draws our gaze outward. Ours is a civilization, it is said, that has forgotten death — death has become an anathema. People try to get by without thinking about or coming into contact with it. But does ignoring death enrich life?

While science can push back the moment of death, it cannot stop it. Death is a condition of human life — no one can escape it. A civilization that has forgotten death, therefore, has forgotten human beings. And a civilization that has forgotten human beings will not bring people happiness.

Tolstoy says: "An enlightened man is he who knows why he lives and what he ought to do. Do not try to be either learned or educated, but strive to become enlightened."[5]

In this sense, aren't the lives of SGI members, who strive to cultivate themselves and serve others based on the eternity of life, enlightened?

There are countless dramas of life and death in the SGI. I have heard of one person who, after expressing gratitude for the SGI, said, "I'll be back soon" and then passed away. Another person, smiling gently, closed her eyes, saying, "I'll be born right away and return to the garden of kosen-rufu." Someone else died after bravely relating his dream — to undertake great activities in his next life — while listening to such well-loved Soka Gakkai tunes as "Song of Comrades" and "The Song of the Human Revolution." Aren't these enlightened people who have awakened to the eternity of life and met death with complete composure?

A civilization that revolves around cultivating life respects human dignity and excellence. It is a society that treasures people of wisdom.

In modern society, where highest value tends to be placed on material wealth and utility, people are often judged on whether they are "useful." As a result, the elderly and the sick tend to be marginalized. A civilization that does not squarely face death also deserts people in sickness and old age. For the rapidly graying populations of many countries, this spells a bleak future.

This would not be the case in a civilization that treasures human maturity and depth of wisdom. If there is value in the young shoots of spring and the light of summer, then there must also be value in the mature trees of autumn and the grand sunsets of winter.

This is all the more so for those who practice Buddhism. For us, old age is a time of unsurpassed fulfillment when we put the finishing touches on the "golden journal" of our lives and attain Buddhahood; days of mission when we show actual proof and relate to others the wonder of life and power of the spirit we have experienced. This lifetime is precious and irreplaceable.

As a young man, the great Russian writer Fyodor Dostoevsky (1821–81) was arrested for revolutionary activities and sentenced to die. He was taken to the execution grounds and, along with his friends, tied to a stake. Guns were pointed at them.

The thought that in a few moments he would no longer be in this world stirred a powerful reaction in the young Dostoevsky. A character from one of his novels in a similar situation thinks to himself:

> What if I were not to die! What if I could go back to life — what eternity! And it would all be mine! I would turn every minute into an age; I would lose nothing, I would count every minute as it passed, I would not waste one![6]

At the last moment the execution was canceled, but the episode left its imprint on Dostoevsky's entire life. His experience might have been extreme, but if we think about things objectively, everyone, differences in length of life notwithstanding, is certain to die. From that standpoint, each of us is a "prisoner on death row."

Incidentally, I understand that efforts are being made to educate people on the subject of death. One example of this is having people imagine that they have only three months to live, encouraging them to think how they would spend that time. This kind of exercise prompts people to think earnestly about what they need to accomplish.

Tolstoy observed:

> If a man knows that he will die inside of thirty minutes, he will not do anything trifling or foolish in these last thirty minutes, surely not anything evil. But is the half century or so that separates you from death essentially different from a half hour?[7]

Use your time wisely and polish your life. When I was young, my health was so poor that I might have died any time. Therefore, I threw myself into efforts for Buddhism with the determination to use each moment to the fullest.

We have to work hard. We have to develop ourselves. As the Daishonin says, "Arouse deep faith and polish your mirror night and day" (MW-1, 5). That is the fundamental objective of life and the conclusion of "The Ultimate Teaching Affirmed by All Buddhas of Past, Present and Future." Daily, we carry out this practice, the essence of Buddhism — this is the same as mastering the eighty-four thousand teachings.

Let us live aware of the fantastic wonder of life, with the realization that each day is a priceless treasure.

1. "Sanze Shobutsu Sokanmon Kyoso Hairyu" (*Gosho Zenshu*, pp. 558–75), written in October 1279 when the Daishonin was 58.

2. Blaise Pascal, *Pensées*, trans. A.J. Krailsheimer (New York: Penguin Books, 1966), pp. 156–57.

3. Michel Eyquem de Montaigne, *The Complete Works of Montaigne*, trans. Donald M. Frame (Stanford, Calif.: Stanford University Press, 1957), p. 196.

4. Leo Tolstoy, *The Pathway of Life*, trans. Archibald J. Wolfe (New York: International Book Publishing Company, 1919), part 2, p. 179.

5. Tolstoy, *The Pathway of Life*, part 1, p. 296.

6. Fyodor Dostoevsky, *The Idiot*, trans. Constance Garnett (New York: Bantam Books, 1988), p. 57.

7. Tolstoy, *The Pathway of Life*, part 2, p. 32.

'Reply to Myoho Bikuni' (1)

A Person of Justice Invites Persecution

Life is a journey. Nichiren Daishonin's entire life was a difficult journey that frequently brought him to the precipice between life and death. As he put it, "As mountains pile upon mountains and waves follow waves, so do persecutions add to persecutions and criticisms augment criticisms" (MW-2 [2ND ED.], 99).

Several men and women accompanied him on that arduous path. From a secular standpoint, they did not benefit in the least from doing so; they were persecuted, badgered and even ridiculed. Yet they maintained their allegiance to the Daishonin, filled with the sense of wonder in being alive at the same time as he.

Life is a journey. Today, those followers who advanced throughout their lives with the Daishonin, the original Buddha, shine with a brilliant hue — as they will throughout eternity.

Myoho Bikuni,[1] the recipient of the letter we will now begin studying,[2] was one such individual. Of all the letters the Daishonin wrote, this is one of the longest. It even has the flavor of a concise autobiography.

This Gosho conveys the sublime spirit of the Daishonin, who continually exerted himself for the people's happiness. This time we will study a portion from the latter half of the letter.

Why are there obstacles? Why is a person of justice persecuted? The Daishonin explains why, illuminating the underlying mechanism at work.

What emerges is the stark contrast between those who continually ask themselves how they should live and those who live by their wits, principally concerned with protecting what they already have.

The Daishonin's Sole Desire: To Protect the People

> My situation is the same [as the T'ang general Li-ju Hsien]. Although I brought forth [this teaching of the True Law] out of the desire to help the people of Japan, I am not allowed even to enter the province of my birth, and now, too, I have left the province of my exile. In living secluded deep in this mountain [Mount Minobu], I resemble Li-ju Hsien.
>
> Since I have no wife or children in either my native province or in my place of exile, there is certainly no need for me to grieve [as Li-ju Hsien must have]. Still, apprehensive thoughts of my parents'

> graves lying untended and of people dear to me weigh on my heart. My feelings are beyond words to express. (*Gosho Zenshu*, p. 1415)

At the start of this passage, the Daishonin refers to an incident during the reign of Chinese emperor Tai-tsung of the T'ang dynasty in the eighth century. A general named Li-ju Hsien had led a great army northward, but his forces were defeated by the enemy and he was taken prisoner. He then spent forty years in captivity. During that time, he took to wearing the region's clothes and even married a local woman and had children.

He was allowed to wear T'ang dress only on New Year's Day. His yearning for his home did not wane so when T'ang forces attacked the land, he approached the T'ang camp alone. Because he was wearing the local people's clothes, though, Li-ju Hsien was mistaken for the enemy and nearly killed.

The opportunity eventually came for him to appeal to the T'ang emperor, Te-tsung, but suspicions still lingered. In the end, he was sent alone into exile to a distant land in the south.

Though he was sincerely patriotic, he could neither see his home nor be with the wife and children he had left behind. What a cruel fate! What grief Li-ju Hsien must have felt!

The Daishonin compares his own situation to Li-ju Hsien's. Although he expounded the Lotus Sutra solely out of the desire to "help the people of Japan," he could not return to his native Awa. And having left Sado Island, his erstwhile place of exile, he was confined to the recesses of Mount Minobu.

In the Daishonin's home province, ruling power was in the hands of Tojo Kagenobu[3] and members of the Hojo family. It appears that they unjustly prohibited him from entering the region.

Of course, the Daishonin never married or had children. Still, he says he is anxious about the condition of his parents' graves and anxious to see people dear to him. When the Daishonin thought about his home, the faces of many friends and relatives must have come to mind. He certainly did not forget people with whom he had formed connections. The Daishonin was a person of such warmth.

At the time, it was common and even regarded as natural for priests to marry. The *Shaseki-shu*,[4] a collection of tales portraying the social conditions of the day, describes such things in detail. It even relates the account of an elderly priest who encouraged all priests he met to marry, so as to have someone to provide for them in old age.

Despite the trend of his times, the Daishonin always conducted himself as a true priest. Nevertheless, society was rife with rumors that he, a man of impeccable integrity, was a "lawless priest," i.e., that he broke the precepts. His bad reputation, based entirely on malicious fabrication, spread far and wide (MW-5, 6). This situation — like that of children striking their parents — was completely absurd.

Through and through, the Daishonin's spirit was to prevent the country from going astray and to help the suffering multitudes. He had profound compassion for the people. But the Japanese not only failed to understand his spirit — they trampled on it.

In taking the actions that he did, the Daishonin was prepared for such reaction. No matter how wise or good people may be, if they fail to fight when it is necessary to do so, they will not attain Buddhahood. They will not achieve victory as human beings. Instead, they will eventually fall into the state of Hell. Nichiren Daishonin fervently upheld the Buddha's admonitions.

Those who don't speak the truth when it is time to may avoid danger. Those who don't take courageous action may live in peace and security. This is probably what wily and cunning people do.

But if someone were trying to kill your parents, you would naturally try to warn them. If someone is clearly about to set out on the wrong path, isn't it one's duty to correct the person? Therefore, the Daishonin urged people to return to the correct path, to go forward along it.

The Daishonin did not expect that those in power would readily accept the truth. He didn't necessarily see them as having the sincerity to be concerned about justice or think about people's well-being. Rather, it was as plain as day to him that by raising the cry to establish the peace of the land through the propagation of the True Law, he would call forth great persecution.

He could not abide in silence. No matter what the outcome, as a Buddhist and a human being, he had no choice but to declare with all truth and honesty what was correct and what was mistaken. Like other "emissaries of the Buddha," he took action "because he treasured the Buddhist Law and did not fear secular rules" (*Gosho Zenshu*, p. 1412). For the sake of truth, he did not fear authority. For precisely that reason, he met with great persecution. That's why, whatever the difficulties the Daishonin faced, the brilliance of his humanity will shine eternally.

Stand-alone Faith Yields Great Benefit

Yet, I feel joy. Although their bodies have perished, the warriors who, true to their ways, marched forward in the cause of their lord, taking the lead in crossing the Uji and Seta rivers,[5] made names that will be known in ages to come.

For the cause of the Lotus Sutra, I, Nichiren, have likewise been driven from my dwelling and attacked on many occasions, suffering wounds on my body. My disciples have been killed. I have twice been condemned to exile in distant regions. And, once, I was almost beheaded. All this I bore for the sake of the Lotus Sutra.

The Buddha preaches in the Lotus Sutra that more than 2,200 years after his death, in the fifth 500-year period [i.e., at the beginning of the Latter Day of the Law] when the Lotus Sutra is about to spread throughout the world, the Devil of the Sixth Heaven will take possession of people, abusing, striking, banishing or killing those who happen to take faith in this sutra, in an attempt to prevent

> them from propagating the sutra's teachings. He goes on to say that those who stand in the vanguard at that time will win benefit as great as though they had given offerings to the Buddhas of the three existences and the ten directions. And the Buddha also promises that he will transfer to such persons the benefits resulting from his own trials and the ascetic practices he underwent as a bodhisattva. (*Gosho Zenshu*, p. 1415)

Why, amid persecution, does the Daishonin say that he feels joy? Just as in battle warriors fight in the front ranks so they can make names for themselves that later generations will remember, the Daishonin stood up in the vanguard of the struggle to propagate the Lotus Sutra.

He says that at the time of kosen-rufu, enemies of the Buddha will appear and persecute the votaries of the Mystic Law. Those who lead the way in the struggle at that time, he asserts, will receive all the benefit that caused Shakyamuni to attain Buddhahood.

It is important to push ourselves to advance on the forefront. It all comes down to self-motivation, conviction and the spirit to stand alone. Those who do activities only because they are told to do so, or out of a sense of obligation, will not experience true joy.

Since we're alive we ought to live with freshness and vigor. If we're going to run, then we should run with all our might. That way we can manifest great strength and realize tremendous benefit.

The Daishonin speaks of the time "when the Lotus Sutra is about to spread throughout the world." That time is truly right now. The sonorous voices of people chanting the Mystic Law can now be heard in 128 countries. This is an age without precedent in Buddhism's history. Right now, we are correctly and profoundly actualizing these words of the Daishonin. What noble lives we are leading!

Nichiren Daishonin explains the reason why he meets obstacles, saying, "This is entirely for the sake of the Lotus Sutra." It is not, he indicates, for any other reason; it is entirely because he is spreading the Mystic Law.

While it might seem that people today are carrying out the same actions, some may be motivated deep down by the desire to protect personal interests. Some may be doing so out of vanity. Some may have calculating minds.

Ultimately it comes down to whether — even if others are not aware of our efforts — we are truly praying and working for kosen-rufu. This difference, while inconspicuous and very subtle, is the decisive factor. And it becomes apparent in whether we attain Buddhahood, whether we realize ultimate victory as human beings.

Buddhism Is Suited to a Global Age

> When in the past Bodhisattva Never Disparaging (Jpn. Fukyo) spread the Law, respected monks and nuns, known for their wisdom and for upholding all 250 rules of the monk's regulations, gathered in a great assembly and cunningly enticed the laymen

and laywomen to slander and attack Bodhisattva Never Disparaging. But Bodhisattva Never Disparaging never thought of turning back and continued to spread the Lotus Sutra, until finally he attained Buddhahood.

Bodhisattva Never Disparaging of the past is the present Shakyamuni Buddha. The respected monks who envied and attacked him fell into the Avichi Hell[6] for a thousand kalpas. Even though they praised thousands of sutras including the Kammuryoju[7] and Amida sutras, hailed the names of all Buddhas, invoked the Nembutsu of Amida Buddha, and day and night read the Lotus Sutra, because they had viewed the true votary of the Lotus Sutra with enmity, neither the Lotus Sutra, nor the Nembutsu teaching nor the precepts could save them, and they fell into the Avichi Hell for a period of a thousand kalpas.

Those monks at first regarded Bodhisattva Never Disparaging with disdain, but later had a change of heart and themselves took action to serve him, following him as slaves would obey their master. Nevertheless, they could not avoid falling into the hell of incessant suffering.

The people of Japan who are now hostile toward Nichiren are the same. No, my situation is completely

> different from that of Bodhisattva Never Disparaging — he was scorned and beaten, but he was never sent into exile by the ruler. He was struck with sticks and staves, tiles and rocks, but he was not wounded or nearly beheaded.
>
> For more than twenty years, I have been continually vilified and attacked by sticks and staves, tiles and rocks. In addition, I have been wounded, exiled, and even nearly beheaded. My disciples have had their lands confiscated, been jailed, sent far away, driven away from their homes, or had their rice paddies and fields stolen. They have been treated even worse than night robbers, thieves, pirates, mountain bandits and rebels. (*Gosho Zenshu*, pp. 1415–16)

Kosen-rufu is a movement to open the eyes of all people to their Buddha nature. In a dialogue that he conducted toward the end of his life, Joseph Campbell (1904–87), an American authority on comparative mythology, remarked:

> When the world changes, then the religion has to be transformed...today there are no boundaries. The only mythology that is valid today is the mythology of the planet — and we don't have such a mythology. The closest thing I know to a planetary mythology is Buddhism, which sees all beings as Buddha beings. The only problem is to come to the recognition of that.[8]

According to Campbell, myths are value systems that give the people of an age or era meaning in life and joy. He identifies Buddhism — which, as he puts it, "sees all beings as Buddha beings" — as the thought system best suited to an age of "one world."

Bodhisattva Never Disparaging perceived the Buddha nature in all people and bowed in reverence to them as he walked along. As a result, people rejected and persecuted him.

No matter how someone may claim to treasure the Law, if he or she persecutes those who spread it, rather than receiving benefit, he or she will be severely punished. Those who persecuted Bodhisattva Never Disparaging later regretted their actions, but they could not avoid retribution for the negative causes they had created.

This was all the more true for those who persecuted Nichiren Daishonin and never even felt remorse for their actions. The Daishonin says, "Even a small error will destine one to the evil paths if one does not repent of it" (MW-4, 164). Not only did they subject the Daishonin to persecutions of an incomparably greater magnitude than those that befell Bodhisattva Never Disparaging, but they never came to regret their actions. In light of the Law of life, their retribution surely defies description.

By contrast, the lives of those who, no matter how they are vilified, thoroughly dedicate themselves to justice are infinitely bright. The sun of hope blazes in their hearts. The followers of Nichiren Daishonin who crossed mountains and rivers together with their mentor were filled with brilliant hope.

Living With Hope

President Josei Toda once said:

> When we consider the lives of great historical figures, we see that without being defeated by the difficulties or hardships of life they steadfastly maintained hope that might seem to ordinary eyes like a dream. Moreover, they lived out their lives without ever abandoning their hopes; they never capitulated.
>
> They could do this, I think, because they were deeply convinced that their hope did not arise from selfish desires or egoism. It was based on a sincere wish for all people's happiness.
>
> From the time the original Buddha, Nichiren Daishonin, at age 16 awoke to the great wish to lead all people to happiness, becoming enlightened to the great truth of the universe, until he reached 32, he engaged in study to confirm his conviction. Thereafter, until the day he died at 61, he never strayed a single step from the hope, the dream, of his youth to which he dedicated his entire life. Reflecting on his life, which represents the realization of this dream, is like gazing upon a magnificent palace....
>
> What I wish most of my comrades, whether they be young or old, is that they will have firm hope in their lives and live with that optimistic spirit. Needless to say, we should

remember that the inner resilience that enables us to live with an unwavering sense of hope and confidence derives from the Gohonzon, which embodies the oneness of the Person and the Law and is the life of Nichiren Daishonin.

Let us plant our feet firmly on the ground and live with brilliant hope. At the same time, let us strive to bring equally bright hope to others and help them gain a solid footing in life.[9]

My mentor lived his entire sublime life in just this way. Nichiren Daishonin teaches the wonder of a life lived with the great aspiration to create a new age in which the people take the lead. Let us advance ever forward, always with our sights on the future.

The great French author Victor Hugo (1802–85) cried: "What is the question of today? It is to fight. What is the question of tomorrow? It is to win."[10]

1. *Bikuni*: A Japanese transliteration of the Sanskrit term *bhikshuni*, meaning "nun."

2. "Myoho Bikuni Gohenji" (*Gosho Zenshu*, pp. 1406–19), written in September 1278 when the Daishonin was 57.

3. Tojo Kagenobu: Steward of Tojo Village in Nagasa District of Awa province. A passionate believer in the Nembutsu.

4. *Shaseki-shu* (Collection of Sand and Pebbles): A work by the Buddhist monk Muju Ichien (1226–1312) in 10 or 12 fascicles, written in 1279. A collection of notes, which reflect the spirit of Buddhism in the Kamakura period, about chance occurrences in daily life.

5. The Uji and Seta rivers were strategic points for defending Kyoto, the capital. They were also the focus of fighting in the struggle between the Minamoto and Taira clans.

6. Avichi Hell: The hell of incessant suffering.

7. The sutra setting forth meditation on Amida Buddha.

8. Joseph Campbell with Bill Moyers, *The Power of Myth*, ed. Betty Sue Flowers (New York: Doubleday, 1988), pp. 21–22.

9. Remarks made on January 1, 1957. Josei Toda, *Toda Josei Zenshu* (Collected Works of Josei Toda) (Tokyo: Seikyo Shimbunsha, 1983), vol. 3, pp. 292–93.

10. Translated from French: Victor Hugo, *Victor Hugo Oeuvres Complètes*, vol. 15 (Paris: Le club français du livre, 1970), p. 1247.

'Reply to Myoho Bikuni' (2)

Courage — The Key to Happiness

When people encounter great obstacles, it's a sure sign they are creating tremendous positive change. This is as true today as it certainly was in Nichiren Daishonin's time.

At the start of 1268, an incident occurred that no one in Japan anticipated. An official letter arrived from the Mongol Empire. Unless Japan did as instructed and submitted to a tributary relationship, the Mongols would attack. People became racked with fear. As the Daishonin says, "Everyone from the ruler above to the people below quaked and trembled with fear" (*Gosho Zenshu*, p. 172). The country was thrown into turmoil; it was as though the world had turned upside down.

Only one person, Nichiren Daishonin, surveyed these events and the great commotion that ensued calmly. The warning that he had made eight years prior in his "Rissho Ankoku Ron"[1] had now become a reality.

This turn of events resulted in a clear change in people's attitudes toward the Daishonin. "This is incredible," people thought. "His teaching must really be correct." From then on, people began chanting daimoku in increasing numbers. In a letter to one believer, the Daishonin says, "Now one tenth of the people in Japan chant only Nam-myoho-renge-kyo" (MW-5, 294).

But it was precisely then, in 1271, that great oppression bore down on the Daishonin with the Tatsunokuchi Persecution — where he was nearly executed by the authorities — and his subsequent exile to Sado Island. That was three-and-a-half years after the arrival of the letter from the Mongols.

Just what had happened? Why did the Daishonin have to encounter such great persecution? This will be the subject of our discussion this time.

Jealous Priests Acting in Collusion with the Authorities

> This [the Daishonin's having encountered persecutions incomparably greater than those which Bodhisattva Never Disparaging faced] is entirely because of the charges made [against the Daishonin to the rulers] by high-ranking priests of the Shingon, Nembutsu and Zen sects.
>
> Accordingly, their offense is more weighty than the earth. Therefore, the earth shakes more violently than a ship on the sea in the midst of a great storm.

The eighty-four thousand stars glare down from the heavens, day and night there are abnormal phenomena in the heavens and the sun and moon also show great irregularities.

Already 2,227 years have passed since the Buddha entered nirvana. Even when King Mihirakula[2] burned all the Buddhist halls and monasteries of the five regions of India and murdered all the monks of the sixteen major states,[3] or when Emperor Wu-tsung[4] of T'ang China destroyed Buddhist temples and pagodas in China and broke up the Buddha images, or when Mononobe no Moriya[5] burned the gilded bronze statue of the Buddha with charcoal and persecuted the monks and nuns, forcing them to return to secular life, never have such comets [as the great comet of 1264] or such great earthquakes [as the great earthquake of 1257] occurred.

The evil of people today is hundreds, thousands, tens of thousands of times more severe. In these earlier cases, the evil mind of a single ruler [was the cause of the persecution]; the persecution did not arise from the hearts of the ministers on down [who merely carried out the king's wishes]. Moreover, King Mihirakula and the others were enemies of the provisional Buddha and sutras. And the monks [who were persecuted] did not practice the Lotus Sutra.

> Now, however, the persecutions are completely against the Lotus Sutra and they represent a great evil spirit that arises not only from the heart of the ruler himself but from the hearts of wise people throughout the entire land and of the entire populace. (*Gosho Zenshu*, p. 1416)[6]

The Daishonin says that scheming was behind the great persecutions that befell him. These attacks arose as a direct result of accusations made against him by respected priests. From various Buddhist schools, priests acting in collusion with government officials leveled accusations against the Daishonin that could not possibly have been true. This was in order to have him done away with.

At the root of this was jealousy. These priests feared people would recognize that the Daishonin was correct. And they alone wanted to have people's respect. They could not match Nichiren Daishonin in debate, though. So even though he sought a public confrontation, they refused to comply.

By rights, these priests ought to have devoted their lives to the well-being of the people, the good of the country and Buddhism itself. Getting caught up in petty emotionalism is a great mistake. But the higher people's standing — when they feel that their position is in jeopardy — the more likely they are to ignore reason and trample on justice.

President Tsunesaburo Makiguchi said:

> Generally speaking, people who pride themselves on being good or extraordinarily good are most concerned

with whether someone superior to them in character may appear. Or whether a method other than theirs will be proven superior. In that case, the higher a person's position, the more directly he or she is destined to make the causes for great or extraordinarily great evil.…

Had Nichiren Daishonin not appeared, then Ryokan,[7] Doryu[8] and others [who were regarded as respected priests by society in the Daishonin's day] would likely have ended their lives revered as living Buddhas. Unfortunately for them, unable to accept the supremacy of the Daishonin's teaching, consumed by concern for their personal interests, they became priests of the greatest evil.[9]

And so, behind the great persecutions that befell the Daishonin were the dark machinations of people jealous of the advance of kosen-rufu, the widespread propagation of the True Law.

The Daishonin describes the mind-set of his persecutors as follows:

When a woman becomes envious, a great fire burns in her heart, and as a result her body turns red. The hair on her body stands on end, her limbs shake and a flame rises to her face, which turns vermilion. Her eyes open wide like the eyes of a cat glaring at a mouse. Her hands tremble, resembling the leaves of an oak blown by the wind. To those nearby, she resembles a great demon.

> This is the state of the ruler and high-ranking priests of Japan, as well as the monks and nuns. When they hear Nichiren declare that the invocation of the Nembutsu to Amida Buddha, on which they rely, leads to the hell of incessant suffering, that Shingon is a teaching that destroys the country and that Zen is the practice of devils, they grind their teeth [in a fit of rage] while counting their prayer beads and bobbing their heads [in exasperation] while ringing their prayer bells.
>
> Although they appear to uphold the precepts, they harbor an evil spirit [to do away with the Daishonin]. Saint Ryokan of Gokuraku-ji temple, who is revered as a living Buddha, has made charges to the government on folded paper [official stationary folded in half]. Saint Doryu of Kencho-ji has ridden on a litter and kneeled before magistrate officials. Nuns of high standing who have received all of the 500 precepts [from Ryokan and others] write their accusations down on the finest silk and present them to high officials. (*Gosho Zenshu*, p. 1416)

The ancient Greek tragedian Euripides (484–06 B.C.E.) characterizes envy as the greatest of human ills. The flames of envy are directed toward others — but the envious person is consumed in the flames.

President Josei Toda said:

> It is a great mistake to suppose that only women are envious. Men are envious, too. In Japanese, the word for envy (*shitto*) [is written with two Chinese characters both containing the element for woman, but it] could just as easily be written using the element for man.... It is often male jealousy that wreaks havoc in the world.[10]

That's right. The envy of evil priests directed toward the Daishonin plunged Japan into turmoil. Ryokan, who reverently presented his slanderous accusations to the government, and Doryu, who rode on a magnificent litter to make his appeals to government officials, groveled before those in power. What shameful hypocrisy they displayed, while passing themselves off as saints!

Why, then, did the government become a willing accomplice in their schemes? There were strong ties between the respected priests and the country's rulers. Ryokan and the others had many influential followers. Also, as the Daishonin indicates, women of high social standing who trusted these priests took action behind the scenes to turn key people in the government against him.

And the country's rulers had their own agendas. In fact, they took advantage of the national crisis, of the impending attack by a foreign power, to quickly expand their sphere of influence. Proclaiming the need to unify the nation to respond to the crisis, officials steadily worked to augment the government's autocratic powers. Those in positions of authority never miss an opportunity to increase their clout.

For example, the ruling Hojo clan used the attack threatened by the Mongols as a pretext to appoint members of their own clan to governorships in provinces throughout western Japan. Even areas where the government's footing had formerly been weak came under Hojo control.

There was an increasing consolidation of power. This government, a military regime to begin with, became increasingly militaristic. Under such circumstances, the government was most aggressive toward people and groups critical of the regime. So it was that Nichiren Daishonin and his followers caught the authorities' attention. Other schools, following the decrees of the government or imperial court, offered prayers for the "defeat of the foreign invaders."

The Daishonin alone cried out that it was useless to offer such prayers; that the prayers offered by adherents of erroneous schools, far from doing any good, would in fact produce an opposite result. His cry struck a chord of sympathy with the people. To the ruling authorities, championing the need to unify the country and concentrate power, nothing could have been more vexing.

From 1268 through 1271, the government's autocratic powers increased. And the Mystic Law also proceeded to spread widely. In other words, the authoritarian government and the rising tide of people seeking justice and peace came head to head. There was a collision between the "top-down" repressive power of the government and the "bottom-up" popular movement critical of that power. This culminated in the Tatsunokuchi Persecution and Sado Exile of 1271.

Certain events illustrate this vividly. The day after the Tatsunokuchi Persecution (which took place on September 12, 1271), the government issued a notice to warriors in the Kanto region, which includes the capital, Kamakura, that those with lands in Kyushu[11] should set out for that domain in all haste to prepare for the Mongol invasion. It instructed them to take measures to defend the realm from the foreign power and also suppress antiestablishment elements within their territories.

That these two events, the Tatsunokuchi Persecution and the notice, took place at exactly the same time was no coincidence. For the government, severe suppression of the Daishonin's followers was part of the strict eleventh-hour policy it had implemented in anticipation of the Mongol invasion.

Behind the imposition of stricter martial law, there was, in addition to the foreign threat, an internal power struggle. As the Hojo clan consolidated its control, conflict with other forces opposed to its dominion grew fierce.

People were filled with suspicion and vied to undercut one another. Thus, even though the leaders appealed to the people to unify the country, embers of civil strife and schisms — the disaster of internal strife that the Daishonin predicted in the "Rissho Ankoku Ron"— smoldered under their feet.

The system of open deliberations that had become a tradition of the Kamakura regime broke down under these circumstances. The affairs of government began to be conducted behind closed doors. Government meetings consisted of important officials of the ruling Hojo clan gathering at the home of the most powerful person of the day. The most important policy decisions were made at such secret councils.

With this system of closed-door government, Hei no Saemon[12] and others who wanted to persecute the Daishonin came to wield tremendous influence as retainers of the Hojo clan. There is a record of the period when Hei no Saemon wielded dictatorial powers that says, "People could not help but live in fear."[13]

In such an authoritarian regime, there is no correct reasoning. Nor is there the compassion to put the people's minds at ease. Self-interest and ambition dominate everything.

Because the government had fallen into such a corrupt state, it was easily moved by the slanderous words of people who hated the Daishonin. The leaders lacked any public accountability, so all it took was a single malicious accusation for them to engineer someone's downfall or death. They may have tried to take a person's life merely because someone else had related there was a rumor about the person going around.

People's hearts were in turmoil. It was a tumultuous age. In the absence of any hope for the future, the sense of foreboding only intensified.

Evil priests took advantage of these conditions to start rumors about the Daishonin. Ordinary people, unaware of the truth, readily believed what they heard.

Even a small lie, through endless repetition, became absurdly exaggerated. People somehow came to accept it as the truth.

This is analogous to how the ingestion of small amounts of poison can gradually and innocuously incapacitate the body, rendering it defenseless. Thus when rumors spread that the Daishonin's disciples were starting fires, people accepted them as true (MW-1, 184).

The behind-the-scenes scheming of evil priests dovetailed with the self-interest of those in power. This resulted in great persecution of the Daishonin. These priests were the very image of the third of the three powerful enemies[14] the Lotus Sutra describes.

Nichiren Daishonin, fully aware of this pattern, dared to enter the maelstrom. In the "Letter From Sado," he says, "When an evil ruler in consort with heretical priests tries to destroy true Buddhism and banish a man of wisdom, those with the heart of a lion will surely attain Buddhahood as Nichiren did" (MW-1, 35). The Daishonin indicates that when great persecution arises, caused by the collusion of an evil ruler and erroneous priests who make slanderous accusations, it represents an opportunity to attain Buddhahood.

We must have the spirit of a lion. The Daishonin says, "The lion fears no other beast" (MW-1, 241). Courage is the absolute condition for attaining Buddhahood. Courage is the absolute condition for becoming happy. President Makiguchi said, "A single lion will triumph over a thousand sheep."[15]

We are direct followers of Nichiren Daishonin, a person of the greatest courage. We have to stand alone with the courageous spirit of lions. Like lions, we have to fight courageously and win the laurel of victory.

1. "Rissho Ankoku Ron" (On Securing the Peace of the Land Through the Propagation of True Buddhism), Nichiren Daishonin's first official remonstration with the

authorities urging them to reject erroneous practices and place their faith in the True Law.

2. Mihirakula: A king of the ancient kingdom of Cheka in India. According to the *Daito Saiiki Ki* (Record of the Western Regions of the Great T'ang Dynasty), he destroyed temples and stupas in many parts of India. As a result, when he was about to die the earth trembled and a storm arose. He fell into the hell of incessant suffering.

3. Sixteen major states: The countries in ancient India — Anga, Magadha, Kashi, Kosala, Vriji, Malla, Chedi, Vatsa, Kuru, Panchala, Ashmaka, Avanti, Matsya, Shurasena, Gandhara and Kamboja.

4. Wu-tsung (814–46): The fifteenth emperor of the T'ang dynasty. In 845 he initiated a sweeping persecution of Buddhism throughout his domains.

5. Mononobe no Moriya (d. 587): An official who opposed the adoption of Buddhism. When an epidemic broke out, he declared it was because of the new religion and attempted to halt all Buddhist practice.

6. "Myoho Bikuni Gohenji" (*Gosho Zenshu*, pp. 1406–19), written in September 1278 when the Daishonin was 57.

7. Ryokan (1217–1303): A priest of the Shingon-Ritsu sect during the Kamakura period (1185–1333).

8. Doryu (1213–78): A priest of the Rinzai sect of Zen, also called Rankei. In 1246, he came to Japan from China. He opposed the Daishonin and, with Ryokan and others, plotted against him.

9. *Makiguchi Tsunesaburo Zenshu* (Collected Writings of Tsunesaburo Makiguchi) (Tokyo: Daisan Bunmeisha, 1987), vol. 10, p. 33.

10. *Toda Josei Zenshu* (Collected Writings of Josei Toda) (Tokyo: Seikyo Shimbunsha, 1988), vol. 8, p. 359.

11. Kyushu: The westernmost of Japan's four major islands, situated closest to the Asian continent.

12. Hei no Saemon (d. 1293): An official of the Hojo regency. He served two successive regents, Hojo Tokimune and Hojo Sadatoki, and wielded tremendous influence in political and military affairs as deputy chief of the Office of Military and Police Affairs. He collaborated with Ryokan and other leading priests to persecute Nichiren Daishonin and his followers.

13. Takayuki Okutomi, *Kamakura Hojoshi no Kisoteki Kenkyu* (Basic Research on the Kamakura Hojo Clan) (Tokyo: Yoshikawa Kobunkan, 1980), p. 229.

14. Priests revered as saints and respected by the general public who, in fear of losing fame or profit, induce the secular authorities to persecute the votaries of the Lotus Sutra.

15. *Makiguchi Tsunesaburo Shingenshu* (A Collection of Tsunesaburo Makiguchi's Sayings), ed. Takehisa Tsuji (Tokyo: Daisan Bummeisha, 1979), pp. 26–27.

'Reply to Myoho Bikuni' (3)

Truth Unwelcome in a Society Pervaded With Lies

Lies erode sanity and distort common sense. Lies are the door to misfortune. They inflict a kind of violence.

Shakyamuni was once asked, "What here [in this world] is the best wealth a person can have?" He answered that the greatest treasure is faith, honest conviction in the truth.[1] This time we will consider how to conduct ourselves in a world where lies are rampant.

> In trying to do away with Nichiren by making slanderous accusations against him, Ryokan and the others while reading the Lotus Sutra fail completely to comprehend it. And while hearing it are utterly deaf to its meaning.
>
> They are drunk on the sweet old sake of the words of Shan-tao[2] and Honen[3] who say that "not one

person in a thousand [can attain Buddhahood through the Lotus Sutra]," or of Kobo[4] and Jikaku[5] who characterize the Lotus Sutra as "just empty theory" or of Bodhidharma[6] who claims that the true teaching of Shakyamuni was transmitted apart from the sutras. As a result, they have become deranged.

For are not people intoxicated who, while seeing the plain statement [in the Lotus Sutra] that the "Lotus is foremost" (LS10, 164), say that the Dainichi Sutra is superior to the Lotus Sutra, or that the teaching of Zen is the supreme Law, or that the Ritsu sect is truly respectworthy or that the Nembutsu is the teaching that actually matches people's capacity?

They are like people who say that stars are superior to the moon, that rocks are superior to gold, that east is west or that the sky is land. Because of their distorted minds, they feel tremendous animosity toward those who tell how things really are and explain that the moon and gold are superior to stars and rocks, that east is east and the sky is the sky.

Under such circumstances, should one blindly follow the majority? Today the majority is just a gathering of many people out of their minds.

I feel the greatest pity for all ordinary men and women who, because they base themselves on this distorted way of thinking, will experience the sufferings of hell. (*Gosho Zenshu*, pp. 1416-17)[7]

Nichiren Daishonin always told things exactly as they were. His actions strictly accorded with the words of Shakyamuni and the sutras. And he never distorted the teachings of the mentor (i.e., Shakyamuni and the Lotus Sutra) to suit his circumstances or because of emotionalism. Truly, in every way his actions mirrored the teachings of Buddhism.

But someone perfectly upright will be detested in a society that is crooked. The *Huai-nan-tzu*, a Chinese classic, contains a saying that something straight cannot be bundled together with a collection of bent objects; similarly, an upright, honest person will not be received in a society where dishonest people hold sway.[8]

Suppose, for instance, that someone repeatedly says the sun rises in the West. Eventually, 999 people out of 1,000 may be brainwashed into believing it as fact. These people are as though intoxicated. Under such circumstances, someone who dissents and asserts that the sun rises in the East will be attacked and persecuted. It is an upside-down society in which falsehood has become endemic.

This was precisely the situation in militarist Japan during the war fifty years ago. Tsunesaburo Makiguchi and Josei Toda, the first and second Soka Gakkai presidents, who appealed for peace and human rights, were accused of being unpatriotic, of being enemies of the country, and they were thrown in prison.

Who were the true winners? The people in power who had these two men imprisoned? The Nichiren Shoshu priests, who sided with the authorities in persecuting them and other practitioners who faithfully followed the Daishonin's teachings? No, they definitely were not.

In an age gone mad, Nichiren Daishonin asked, "Should one blindly follow the majority?" With this question, he deftly exposed the tendency of the Japanese to blindly submit to the will of others.

In this letter, the Daishonin says of the propagation of the Pure Land, or Nembutsu teaching, "People, without giving careful consideration [to whether the teaching is correct], took faith in the Nembutsu one after another because it is easy to practice" (*Gosho Zenshu*, p. 1410).

Has the spiritual climate of Japan, the tendency of the Japanese to be carried away by the current of the times, changed over the centuries? Have the people of Japan developed the wisdom to reject lies and deception?

Japanese society is said to be one of the few essentially non-religious societies in the world. The great Russian author Leo Tolstoy (1828–1910) said: "The religion of those who do not recognize religion is to follow everything the powerful majority does. Simply put, it is the religion of submission to those currently in power."[9] This is truly a profound insight. Tolstoy put his finger on Japanese society's fundamental ailment.

Unless people possess firm conviction in their hearts — unless they can honestly say to themselves, "I will never compromise on this point" and, "I will stake my life on defending this ideal" — they will be swayed, unable to resist the pressures of the majority. And of course it will then be even more difficult for them to endure persecution at the hands of the authorities.

Ultimately, such people, in everything they do, will follow the powerful majority. They will have a wait-and-see attitude and take whatever action is expedient at the moment. With the hollow justification that "there's no other way," they will time and again capitulate to those in power.

As an example, we can cite Japan's collapse fifty years ago as a result of the Japanese people's inability to resist the current of the times and their repeated deferment to precedent. When Japan was in such dire straits, who risked their lives to raise a truly patriotic cry? Wasn't it Tsunesaburo Makiguchi and Josei Toda?

The Soka Gakkai is now changing the spiritual climate of Japan. The only way is to empower and enlighten the people. Unless people gain the ability to see the essence of things for themselves, Japan will be condemned again to go down the slope of decline. I do not think I am alone in my concern for Japan's future.

Nichiren Daishonin was treated as an enemy by thirteenth-century Japan. Many groundless, defamatory rumors were spread about him. Yet despite relentless persecution, he courageously waged a lone struggle against great odds. "There are legions of enemies opposing the single king of the Law [Nichiren] and the handful who follow him," he says (MW-1, 101).

But even though he was virtually alone, the Daishonin was calm and composed. He gazed down, as though from the sky above, on the events enveloping him as though they were illuminated by the brilliant sun of truth.

The Soka Gakkai, given the many great difficulties that have beset it, would likewise have fallen apart long ago if it were fraudulent or fake. But because we dedicate ourselves to the truth and because we are not dishonest, we resolutely face whatever challenges confront us without being alarmed or shaken in the least.

A Brilliant Struggle, a Triumphant Life

In the Nirvana Sutra, the Buddha says that in the Latter Day of the Law those who slander the Lotus Sutra and fall into hell will be more numerous than the dust particles that comprise the earth, while those who believe in the Lotus Sutra and become Buddhas will be fewer than the specks of dirt one can pile on a fingernail.

You should consider things in light of these words. Is it possible that the people of Japan correspond to the specks of dirt on a fingernail and the one person Nichiren to the dust particles [of the worlds] in the ten directions?

Nonetheless, what karmic relationship could have caused you and your sister-in-law to send me a robe? Your making of such an offering surely indicates your desire to join those who count themselves among the specks of dirt that can be placed on a fingernail.

The Nirvana Sutra also says that even though one might be able to dangle a thread from the Brahma heaven in a great wind and thread it through the eye of a needle set upon the earth, it is extremely difficult to encounter the votary of the Lotus Sutra in the Latter Day of the Law.

The Lotus Sutra tells of a turtle that lives at the bottom of the sea. Once every three thousand years the turtle rises to the surface. At that time, if he happens to find a hollowed-out sandalwood log, he can rest in its hollow to cool his belly while warming his back in the sun. Because the turtle is one-eyed and squint-eyed, he sees west as east and east as west. [And even if he is fortunate enough to find a log shaped just right, he may be unable to climb into its hollow (LS27, 315).]

These examples illustrate just how rare the men and women born in the evil age of the Latter Day are who can thread themselves through the needle's eye or rest in the hollow of the Lotus Sutra and Nam-myoho-renge-kyo. (*Gosho Zenshu*, p. 1417)

Shakyamuni once took a pinch of dirt and placed it on his fingernail. Pointing out that the dirt could easily fall off because of its precarious position, he asked his disciple Mahakashyapa, "Which is greater, the amount of dirt on this fingernail or the amount of dirt of the worlds in the ten directions?"

Mahakashyapa replied, "The amount of dirt of the worlds in the ten directions is of course incomparably greater than the amount of dirt on your fingernail."

"That's right," Shakyamuni said, nodding. "Although people are fortunate enough to have been born as human beings, those who persevere in following the correct path and attain the Buddha's state of life are comparable to the specks of dirt that can be placed on a fingernail. Whereas those who deviate from the correct path and fall into an evil path are comparable to the dust particles of the worlds in the ten directions."[10]

There are two paths in life: correct and evil. One path deviates from the state of life of eternal happiness and descends into misery. That is the life of those who fall into the category of "dust particles of the earth" — it is a state of inexorable downward momentum, just as in gravity pulling everything down to earth. The other path is of those who embrace the Mystic Law throughout their lives and ascend the slope of limitless growth and advance. It is a positive life of upward momentum — a life of struggling against the gravitational force of decline and defeat to soar vibrantly into the blue skies of happiness. It is the life of having a place among the "specks of dirt on a fingernail."

Nichiren Daishonin thus assures Myoho Bikuni that she is following the supreme way of life.

Even after the Daishonin was no longer in Kamakura and had retired to Mount Minobu, persecution continued. The storm of oppression against Shijo Kingo, the Ikegami brothers and other followers in the capital grew fierce. The priest

Ryokan of Gokuraku-ji tried in various ways to pressure key figures among the Daishonin's followers to abandon faith.

In the Suruga region, present-day Shizuoka Prefecture, authorities lay in wait for any chance to destroy the community of the Daishonin's followers. This culminated in the Atsuhara Persecution in 1279, the year after this letter was written. But signs of the impending attack were already evident in 1278.

In April 1278, there was a rumor in Kamakura that the Daishonin would be exiled for a third time. Under these circumstances, Myoho Bikuni determined to advance with the Daishonin and take action on his behalf. And she was not alone in cherishing this resolve. Her determination was shared by the wife of her elder brother. This sister-in-law made an offering to the Daishonin of a robe (*Gosho Zenshu*, p. 1406).

It is a marvel that they possessed such sincerity, such faith, even while surrounded by persecutors of the Daishonin as numerous as "the dust particles of the earth." The Daishonin praises both of them and attributes their faith to a profound karmic relationship. It was a karmic relationship with the Daishonin that impelled them to act as they did; there was nothing coincidental about it.

Encountering the Mystic Law is even more difficult than dangling a thread from heaven to earth in a strong wind and threading it through the eye of a needle. It is more difficult than for a one-eyed turtle to find a piece of floating wood in the middle of the ocean with a hollow in it just the right size to enter.

We have the rare good fortune to have been born at this time of unprecedented kosen-rufu. This is due to a profound and unbreakable karmic relationship. Our mission is ever so profound! The important thing, therefore, is that we always continue to uphold the Mystic Law and realize ultimate victory in our lives.

The Daishonin says, "One who perseveres through great persecution and embraces the sutra from beginning to end is the Buddha's emissary" (MW-3, 290). At times of great persecution, we must summon forth strong faith, chant resolute daimoku and speak out for justice. We have to offer prayers with the spirit to squarely face the persecution and struggle selflessly. Those who do so will become Buddhas. They correspond to the "specks of dirt on a fingernail."

Cultivating Good Relations Equals the Key to Happiness

> What karma or relation from the past could have made you want to present an offering to this person [Nichiren]? When we read the Lotus Sutra, we find it explains that this spirit arises in a person when Shakyamuni Buddha enters his or her life.
>
> This is comparable to how when someone becomes drunk on sake an unexpected spirit may arise in them and they may want to give things away to others, even though they previously had no such inclination. Thus, someone who would otherwise fall into the world of Hunger on account of stinginess and greed may, through the external cause of sake, be possessed by the spirit of a bodhisattva.

Dirty water becomes clear when a jewel is placed in it. When a person faces the moon his or her mind begins to wander.

A demon depicted in a painting has no spirit, but is still frightening. A courtesan in a painting cannot steal your husband, but it can still elicit envy. One will not want to enter even fine brocade bedding if the image of a snake is woven into it. When we feel hot, a warm breeze is unpleasant.

The same is true of people's minds. Since you are a woman who devotes herself to the Lotus Sutra, it must be that the dragon king's daughter[11] has entered your heart. (*Gosho Zenshu*, pp. 1417–18)

The mind changes in response to external causes or relations. The examples the Daishonin gives are superb. A spirit like the bodhisattva spirit may, on account of drink, even manifest in a person ordinarily not inclined to be charitable, prompting him or her to give things to others. Just viewing the painting of a demon can arouse fear.

Our lives are determined by the relations we form. And the SGI is a cluster of relations of the very best kind. In a society pervaded with cruel relations, where many people delight in others' misfortunes, we can find, with our fellow members, the greatest solidarity and peace of mind. We have to resolutely protect the noble gathering of the SGI members.

The most important relationship we form in life is with a mentor. None are happier or more fortunate than those who advance with their mentor. I have reached my fiftieth year of practice; I joined the Soka Gakkai on August 24, 1947. On an evening ten days prior, I met my mentor, Josei Toda, for the first time. Mr. Toda was 47 and I was 19.

Half a century has passed. I have given myself totally to fulfilling my destiny in this lifetime in which I have encountered the Mystic Law — which is so difficult to encounter — and have had the great fortune of meeting so rare and exceptional a mentor. I have thoroughly dedicated myself to the path of the oneness of mentor and disciple.

There have been days of storms, violent winds and raging seas. Still, I can say with full conviction that these fifty years of living with President Toda have been days of unsurpassed happiness. During these fifty years with my beloved, courageous fellow Bodhisattvas of the Earth, I have made Nichiren Daishonin's will of kosen-rufu a reality. And these fifty years, as a true disciple of the Daishonin, I have won completely in the continuous struggle against the great hardships that the Gosho predicts the Mystic Law's practitioners will face. My life is completely free of regret, like a cloudless blue sky.

And I will continue to advance, to struggle — solely out of the hope for the growth and dynamic advance of the youth. I will continue single-mindedly advancing for kosen-rufu, to fulfill the vow that I made to President Toda and open a brilliant path for all of you.

*The journey to spread the Mystic Law is long,
Yet encouraging each other,
We continue onward hand in hand.*

In accordance with these lines composed by President Toda, let us ever continue advancing in eternal unity.

1. *The Book of the Kindred Sayings*, a translation of the *Sanyutta-nikaya* (Grouped Suttas) by Mrs. Rhys Davids (Oxford: Pali Text Society 1993), p. 59.

2. Shan-tao (613–81): Third patriarch of the Chinese Pure Land school.

3. Honen (1133–1212): Founder of the Japanese Pure Land school.

4. Kobo (774–835): Third patriarch of the Japanese Shingon school.

5. Jikaku (794–866): Third patriarch of the Japanese Tendai school.

6. Bodhidharma (sixth century): Founder of the Chinese Ch'an (Jpn. Zen) school.

7. "Myoho Bikuni Gohenji" (*Gosho Zenshu*, pp. 1406–19), written in September 1278 when the Daishonin was 57.

8. Liu An (d. 122 B.C.E.), *Huai-nan-tzu*.

9. Translated from Japanese: *Torusutoi Zenshu* (Complete Works of Tolstoy), trans. Toru Nakamura (Tokyo: Kawade Shobo Shinsha, 1974), vol. 15, pp. 135–36.

10. Sutra of the Great Nirvana, vol. 33.

11. Dragon king's daughter: Daughter of Sagara, one of the eight dragon kings said to dwell in a palace at the bottom of the sea. According to "Devadatta," the twelfth chapter of the Lotus Sutra, she conceived the desire for enlightenment when she heard Bodhisattva Monjushiri preach the Lotus Sutra in the dragon king's palace. Later, she appeared before the assembly at Eagle Peak and attained enlightenment immediately, without changing her form.

'Happiness in This World'

We Practice Faith To Become Truly Happy

We practice faith to fully enjoy life, to lead the happiest possible existence. The Gosho we will study this time, "Happiness in This World,"[1] explains the "secret teaching" that makes this possible. It is a short letter, but it offers a complete exposition of the ultimate principles of faith. When we deeply understand this Gosho, we have internalized the secret of faith and of life.

> There is no greater happiness for human beings than chanting Nam-myoho-renge-kyo. The sutra says, "The people there [in my land] are happy and at ease."[2] "Happy and at ease" here means the joy derived from the Law. You are obviously included among the "people," and "there" indicates the entire world, which includes Japan. "Happy and at ease" means to know that our lives — both our bodies and minds, ourselves

and our surroundings — are the entities of *ichinen sanzen* and the Buddha of absolute freedom. There is no greater happiness than having faith in the Lotus Sutra. It promises us "peace and security in this life and good circumstances in the next."[3] Never let life's hardships disturb you. After all, no one can avoid problems, not even saints or sages.

Just chant Nam-myoho-renge-kyo, and when you drink sake, stay at home with your wife. Suffer what there is to suffer, enjoy what there is to enjoy. Regard both suffering and joy as facts of life and continue chanting Nam-myoho-renge-kyo, no matter what happens. Then you will experience boundless joy from the Law. Strengthen your faith more than ever.

With my deep respect,

Nichiren

The twenty-seventh day of the sixth month in the second year of Kenji (1276). (MW-1, 161–62)

Chanting Nam-myoho-renge-kyo Equals the Greatest Happiness

There is no greater happiness for human beings than chanting Nam-myoho-renge-kyo.

"Human beings" at the outset carries great significance. This means all humankind; the Daishonin's teaching can benefit all people without exception.

Buddhism is a teaching that exists for all human beings. It is not only for the Japanese or the people of one particular country or ethnic group. Nichiren Daishonin declares that, ultimately, for all people — whether poor or wealthy, famous or unknown, powerful individuals or ordinary citizens, artists or scientists — apart from chanting Nam-myoho-renge-kyo, there is no true happiness, no true joy or fulfillment in life. That's because when we chant daimoku, our lives become one with the life of the Buddha, enabling us to draw forth the inexhaustible strength to carry out our human revolution and to help others do the same.

Fame, wealth and social status alone do not guarantee happiness. Many wealthy individuals suffer terribly within their mansions. Some people may be so bound up in vanity that they can find no peace of mind. Many famous people feel miserable the moment they slip from the limelight.

Let's say there are two people who work in the same company, perform identical jobs and have equivalent material resources and social standing; yet one feels happy while the other feels nothing but despair. It is not at all uncommon to find such disparities among people whose lives are otherwise quite similar. The disparities arise due to differences in people's inner states, differences in their hearts.

Nor can it be said that the advance of science or economics necessarily brings happiness. In every case, whether we feel happy or unhappy ultimately depends on us. Without changing our state of life, we can find no true happiness. But when we do change our inner state, our entire world is transformed. The ultimate means for effecting such change is chanting daimoku.

> The sutra says, "The people there [in my land] are happy and at ease."

This sutra passage is from the *jigage* section of the "Life Span" chapter of the Lotus Sutra. It means that in this world people ought to live in happiness and ease. We recite this passage every morning and evening in gongyo.

We are born in this world to enjoy life. We are not born to suffer. This is the basic premise of the Lotus Sutra on the nature of human existence. To live happy and at ease in this world means to enjoy our work and family life, to enjoy helping others through Buddhist activities. If we have a truly high state of life, then even when unpleasant things happen we view them as making life all the more interesting, just as a pinch of salt can actually improve the flavor of a sweet dish. We feel true delight in life, whatever happens.

This sutra passage assures us that we can definitely develop such a great life force. And it urges us to exert ourselves in Buddhist practice toward that end.

> "Happy and at ease" here means the joy derived from the Law.

To experience the "joy derived from the Law" means to fully savor the eternally unchanging Mystic Law and the power and wisdom that derive from it. In contrast to this joy, there is the "joy derived from desires" — the enjoyment that comes from fulfilling desires of various kinds. While it might seem like genuine happiness, such joy is only temporary and superficial. It does not arise from the depths of our lives and it soon gives way to unhappiness and dissatisfaction.

Faith enables us to receive the eternal joy derived from the Law. So let us engrave in our hearts this point: We ourselves receive this joy. Because we receive it ourselves, our happiness does not depend on others. No one else can make us happy. Only by our own efforts can we become happy.

Therefore, there is no need to feel envious of others. There is no need to bear a grudge against someone or depend on another person for our happiness. Everything comes down to our state of life. It is within our power to take our lives in any direction we wish.

To be dragged around by other people or the environment is not the way of life the Lotus Sutra teaches. True happiness is not feeling happiness one moment and misery the next. Rather, overcoming the tendency to blame our sufferings on others or on the environment enables us to greatly expand our state of life.

Also, at the most fundamental level, faith is for our sake, not for anyone else's. While we of course practice for ourselves and others and to realize kosen-rufu, ultimately we are the prime beneficiaries of all our efforts in faith. Everything is for our growth; everything contributes to the development of our state of life and the establishment of Buddhahood in our lives. When we practice with this determination, all complaints vanish. The world of Buddhahood that had been covered by the dust of complaints begins to shine, and we can freely and fully savor the joy deriving from the Law.

True 'Peace and Security' Is Having Courage to Overcome Hardships

> You are obviously included among the "people," and "there" indicates the entire world, which includes Japan. "Happy and at ease" means to know that our lives — both our bodies and minds, ourselves and our surroundings — are the entities of *ichinen sanzen* and the Buddha of absolute freedom.

The Daishonin says that this passage, "The people there [in my land] are happy and at ease," is about each of us. The sad thing is that no matter how much we read the sutra or study the Gosho, we still have the tendency to think, "That might be true for others, but my situation is different." Particularly, when we are assailed by storms of adversity, when it seems as though our hearts will burst with woe, we may think, "Only *my* sufferings are beyond help." But in this passage the Daishonin tells us that this definitely is not the case.

When this letter was written, Shijo Kingo, its recipient, had been libelously accused of various wrongs by his colleagues and had fallen from favor with his lord as a result. This was all due to envy. Kingo had enjoyed the deep trust of his lord, but he also had the straightforwardness to speak out when he felt it necessary. As a result, he had made many enemies.

People have the tendency to become envious over the slightest thing, which is perhaps human nature. They may try to undercut someone of whom they feel envious and then delight at the person's misfortune. We must not be defeated by this pitiful tendency. To allow ourselves to become caught up in or swayed by such whirlpools of emotion, going from elation one moment to dejection the next, is pointless.

As indicated by the phrase "[receiving oneself] the joy derived from the Law," the key is to develop such inner strength that we can look upon everything from the world of Buddhahood, the condition of supreme happiness. And, as the Daishonin says, steadfastly chanting daimoku enables us to do this.

Also, as the Daishonin indicates where he speaks of "both our bodies and minds, ourselves and our surroundings," Buddhism is not abstract theory involving only the mind. Nor is it about changing our subjective outlook irrespective of other people and our surroundings.

The good fortune and benefit we accumulate in the depths of our lives become manifest on the material plane, as well as in our environment. In our bodies and minds, ourselves and our surroundings, it is the mind of faith, which is invisible, that moves everything with enormous power and strength in the best possible direction — toward happiness, toward the fulfillment of all our wishes.

Someone who puts this principle into practice is a "Buddha of absolute freedom." Leaving aside a doctrinal discussion of this term, the Buddha of absolute freedom is a Buddha who, while remaining an ordinary person, freely receives and uses limitless joy derived from the Law.

Specifically, the Buddha of absolute freedom is Nichiren Daishonin. In a general sense, the term also refers to those striving to achieve kosen-rufu who have a direct connection in faith to the Daishonin.

"Absolute freedom" is interpreted by the Daishonin as meaning "the property to freely receive and use." In one place he says:

> The "property to freely receive and use" is the principle of a single life-moment possessing three thousand realms. (*Gosho Zenshu*, p. 759)

Josei Toda explained that the Gohonzon is an inexhaustible store of benefit. And Nichikan declared, "[If only you take faith in this Gohonzon and chant Nam-myoho-renge-kyo even for a while,] no prayer will go unanswered, no offense will remain unforgiven, all good fortune will be bestowed and all righteousness proven."[4]

The extent to which we can receive and use the vast, profound joy derived from the Law depends entirely on our faith. Will we take only a small cup of water from the ocean, or will we fill up a large swimming pool? Can we freely receive and use still more? This is determined entirely by faith.

If somewhere in your heart you have decided, "I alone am incapable of becoming happy," "Only I cannot become a capable person" or, "Only my sufferings will forever remain unresolved," then that one factor of your mind or determination will obstruct your benefit.

In this passage, therefore, the Daishonin's intention is to tell Shijo Kingo, who was experiencing great hardship, "You, too, definitely can become happy just as the sutra states." The Daishonin expresses his immense compassion here.

> There is no greater happiness than having faith in the Lotus Sutra. It promises us "peace and security in this life and good circumstances in the next."

There is a saying, "A small heart gets used to misery and becomes docile, while a great heart towers above misfortune." True happiness is not the absence of suffering; you cannot have day after day of clear skies. True happiness lies in building a self that stands dignified and indomitable like a great palace — on all days, even when it is raining, snowing or stormy.

Attaining "peace and security in this life" doesn't mean having a life free from all difficulties, but that whatever difficulties arise, without being shaken in the least, you can summon up the unflinching courage and conviction to fight against and overcome them. This is the state of life of "peace and security in this life."

And, as indicated by the dictum, "If you want to understand what results will be manifested in the future, look at the causes that exist in the present,"[5] establishing a great state of happiness and security in this life is proof that in the future you will experience good circumstances; being born into a place conducive to your further growth.

Some religions teach that people will become happy after death even if their present lives are filled with misery. But this is not the teaching of the Lotus Sutra, which explains that we can thoroughly enjoy both the present and the future. That is the essence of Buddhism.

Toward establishing such an existence, we need to develop a strong life force by chanting daimoku and thoroughly challenging the realities of our lives. It is through such efforts that we realize true "peace and security in this life" and "good circumstances in the next."

'Regard Both Suffering and Joy As Facts of Life'

Never let life's hardships disturb you. After all, no one can avoid problems, not even saints or sages.

Not even saints and sages, the Daishonin says, can avoid difficulties. In society, people tend to suppose that if someone is vilified and persecuted, the person must be somehow bad or evil. But from the standpoint of Buddhism, it is possible that people may be verbally attacked and undergo difficulties even though they are without guilt or blame. People may label or write about a good person as though evil, assert that lies are true and depict the truth as a lie. This is a fact of human society.

Shijo Kingo, too, suffered on account of calumny. But the Daishonin told him, "Never let life's hardships disturb you." Those who resort to libelous accusations are defeated as human beings; nothing is more lowly and base. We should not be swayed in the least by such despicable actions. Just as we do not put garbage into our mouths, we must not permit such rubbish into our hearts. The Daishonin in effect encouraged

Shijo Kingo to shut the cowardly behavior of his accusers out of his mind. The Roman philosopher Seneca (4 B.C.E.?–C.E. 65) says that the arrows of slander cannot pierce the heart of a person of wisdom.[6]

Much human misery arises from people despairing over things that despairing cannot help. We should not worry about things that no amount of worrying will resolve. The important thing is to build a golden palace of joy in our hearts that nothing can disturb — a state of life like a clear blue sky above the storm, an oasis in the desert, a fortress looking down on high waves.

What matters most is that we fight thoroughly against injustice with a lofty, dauntless spirit. While waging a determined struggle against evil that nearly cost him his life, Nichiren Daishonin cried out [to Shijo Kingo, as they were being led to the execution grounds at Tatsunokuchi], "You should be delighted at this great fortune" (MW-1, 181). And he wholeheartedly anticipated that his disciples would "form their ranks and follow him" (MW-1, 176).

Even a tiny speck of evil that causes people to be unhappy should not be tolerated. Attaining "peace and security in this life and good circumstances in the next" lies precisely in carrying out such a struggle with the faith of indomitable courage.

> **Just chant Nam-myoho-renge-kyo, and when you drink sake, stay at home with your wife.**

The moment he set foot outside his home, Shijo Kingo was in danger of being attacked by enemies. The Daishonin cautions him not to act with imprudence but to stay at home and chant daimoku. And he advises that Shijo Kingo and his wife encourage one another. He taught his follower, in other words, the importance of faith for building a happy, harmonious family.

The Daishonin urged Shijo Kingo to live happily in the present, without brooding on events of the past or needlessly troubling himself over what might happen in the future. Happiness does not lie far off in the distance. It is to be found in the here and now.

> Suffer what there is to suffer, enjoy what there is to enjoy. Regard both suffering and joy as facts of life and continue chanting Nam-myoho-renge-kyo, no matter what happens. Then you will experience boundless joy from the Law.

In times of suffering, chant daimoku. In times of joy, chant daimoku. Chanting daimoku is itself happiness. In life, there are both times of suffering and of joy. These are all irreplaceable scenes in life's drama. Without suffering, we could not appreciate joy. Without tasting the flavors of both suffering and joy, we could not savor life's profundity.

"Suffer what there is to suffer," the Daishonin says. Suffering is inevitable in life. Therefore, we need to be prepared for hardship and to have the inner fortitude to rise above our worries and anxieties. We have to cause the "serene light of the moon of enlightenment" (*Gosho Zenshu*, p. 1262) — the world of Buddhahood — to shine in our lives. Then earthly desires are transformed into enlightenment and we can use everything that happens in life to fuel our happiness.

To "enjoy what there is to enjoy" means to cause the "mystic lotus of the heart" (*Gosho Zenshu*, p. 978) to brightly blossom with a sense of appreciation and joy. Someone who can find joy, who can feel appreciation, experiences a snowballing exhilaration and joy in life. Such is the heart's function.

The ocean, even when waves are crashing on its surface, is calm and unchanging in its depths. There is both suffering and joy in life — the point is to develop a profound, indomitable self not influenced by these waves. A person who does so receives the joy derived from the Law.

In the journey of kosen-rufu things will not always proceed smoothly. But we are eternal comrades. People who come together in good times but desert one another when the going gets rough are not comrades. Turning a blind eye to the sufferings of others, using the rationale that "it has nothing to do with me," is not the spirit of comrades. True comrades share both suffering and joy.

We suffer together, rejoice together and bring our lives to fruition together. We regard both suffering and joy as facts of life and continue chanting Nam-myoho-renge-kyo, no matter what happens. To maintain this comradeship, this single-minded commitment to faith, is our eternal guideline in advancing toward kosen-rufu. Let us ever advance with the strong unity of faith!

Strengthen your faith more than ever.

When Nichiren Daishonin was taken to be executed at Tatsunokuchi, Shijo Kingo ran straight to his side. Clutching the reins of the horse on which the Daishonin rode, he resolutely stood by him, vowing to kill himself and join him in death. He was a person of immensely strong faith who boldly ran forward along the path of mentor and disciple.

Even to Shijo Kingo, who possessed such strong faith, the Daishonin says, "Strengthen your faith more than ever." It's not a matter of what we've done in the past — it's what we do from now on that counts. Strength of faith is what everything comes down to. Faith is strength. It is the greatest power people have.

We receive the power of the Buddha and power of the Law embodied in the Gohonzon in accordance with the power of our faith and practice. Faith is the secret art for thoroughly infusing our daily lives with the inherent power of the universe.

Shijo Kingo exerted himself in faith just as the Daishonin instructed. After his difficulties passed, he showed actual proof by regaining the firm trust of his lord and having the size of his lands doubled. Those colleagues who harassed him suffered pitiful consequences.

To practice just as the Daishonin instructs is the fundamental spirit of the SGI. We are advancing in strict accord with the Gosho's teachings. As long as we remember this point, we can definitely achieve great victory in life and our efforts for kosen-rufu.

The Gosho is truly an eternal teaching, which we should be most grateful to have. Thanks to our having encountered this teaching, we can lead wonderful lives of eternal victory.

1. "Shijo Kingo Dono Gohenji" (*Gosho Zenshu*, p. 1143), written in June 1276 when the Daishonin was 55.

2. LS16, 230.

3. LS5, 99.

4. From his "Commentary on 'The True Object of Worship.'"

5. From Shakyamuni's Shinjikan Sutra. See MW-2 [2ND ED.], 172.

6. Seneca: *Moral Essays*, trans. John W. Basore (Cambridge, MA: Harvard University Press, 1958), vol. 1, pp. 57–59.